Corporate Social Responsibility:
A Guide, with Irish Experiences

Corporate Social Responsibility: A Guide, with Irish Experiences

Sheila Killian

Chartered Accountants Ireland

Published by
Chartered Accountants Ireland
Chartered Accountants House
47–49 Pearse Street
Dublin 2
www.charteredaccountants.ie

ISBN: 978-1-907214-63-9

Typeset by Datapage
Printed by Turners Printing Company, Longford

To John, Finn, Cian and Aoife

Contents

Table of Exhibits   *xi*
Foreword, by Michael D. Higgins, President of Ireland   *xiii*
Preface   *xv*
Acknowledgements   *xix*

PART 1   THE THEORY

Chapter 1   **The Meaning of 'Corporate Social Responsibility'**   **3**
'Corporate'   3
'Responsibility'   3
'Social'   4
'Corporate Social Responsibility'   5
The 'Triple Bottom Line'   6
Corporate Citizenship   6
Corporate Responsibility   7
Sustainability   7
Practice   8

Chapter 2   **The Business and Moral Arguments**   **11**
Introduction   11
The 'Moral Case'   12
The 'Business Case'   15

Chapter 3   **Some of the History behind 'CSR'**   **17**
The Modern Debate about CSR   20
Trends in CSR Implementation   22

Chapter 4   **What are the Responsibilities of a Business?**   **27**
1. Economic Responsibilities   27
2. Environmental Responsibilities   31
3. Responsibilities to the Local Community   35
4. Responsibilities to Employees, and Human Rights   39

5. Governance Responsibilities – Combating Corruption 42
6. Product Safety and Quality 45
7. Responsibilities for the Supply Chain 45
8. Taking Responsibility for a Cause, and
   Cause Marketing 49
Conclusion 53

Chapter 5   Standards and Regulation   54
The United Nations Global Compact 55
The Global Reporting Initiative 56
GRI in Action 59
SA8000 60
The International Organisation for Standardisation 60
Other Standards 61

Chapter 6   Reporting on CSR   63
Advantages of External CSR reporting 63
Forms of External CSR Reports 64
Conclusion 69

Chapter 7   CSR in Smaller Enterprises   70
The Importance of Responsibility in SMEs 70
Why Smaller Firms do not Report CSR 71
Why SMEs Should Report 75
Responsibilities of Smaller Firms 76
Conclusion 78

Chapter 8   The Future of CSR   79
Conclusion 86

Part II   The Practice – Irish Experiences of CSR

Introduction to Part II   91

Case A   The Printer   93

Case B   The Mine   99

Case C   The Bookshop   107

Case D   The Coffee Shop and Surf School   113

Case E   The HR Consultants   119

Case F   The Outdoor Centre   125

Case G   The Hotel   131

Case H   The School Lunch Provider   137

References and Resources   143

Index   147

Table of Exhibits

Exhibit 1 – Stakeholders   5

Exhibit 2 – Ideas on Business Ethics   12

Exhibit 3 – Cadbury – Changing through Time   18

Exhibit 4 – Partnering with Non-governmental
        Organisations (NGOs)   23

Exhibit 5 – Pricing Responsibly   28

Exhibit 6 – Taxation   30

Exhibit 7 – Carbon Credits   32

Exhibit 8 – Business in the Community Ireland (BITCI)   38

Exhibit 9 – Business and Human Rights   41

Exhibit 10 – Transparency International   44

Exhibit 11 – Pinkwashing   50

Exhibit 12 – Changing Standards Geographically   57

Exhibit 13 – Signalling Theory Applied   64

Exhibit 14 – European Examples of SME Engagement
        with CSR   74

Exhibit 15 – Trust   79

Exhibit 16 – CSR as Evolution   82

Exhibit 17 – Changing Culture at Interface Carpets   84

Foreword

UACHTARÁN NA hÉIREANN
PRESIDENT OF IRELAND

MESSAGE FROM PRESIDENT MICHAEL D. HIGGINS

I am delighted to send warm greetings on the publication of this book on Corporate Social Responsibility focusing on smaller Irish companies.

It is so worthwhile to create a business publication with its focus on social values, the values that drive smaller firms to provide services for local communities – from actual service-provision to people management within the firms. This book strives to heighten awareness about the responsibility to raise standards in business. It offers guidance in addressing human rights issues and discusses the benefit of engaging in community partnership, which in turn draws on the rich body of knowledge waiting to be tapped in this area. Once again education is seen to promote the concept of social responsibility in the corporate sector, and I commend your efforts to win the hearts and minds of businesses, small and large, and to bring these concepts to the fore.

My very best wishes in all of your endeavours.

Michael D. Higgins
Uachtarán na hÉireann
President of Ireland

Preface

"If we could get the hang of it entirely/It would take too long"
Louis MacNeice ("Entirely")

Corporate social responsibility (CSR) has never been more in the news. Everyone, it seems, has a view on the irresponsible lenders, borrowers, investors and traders who are variously held responsible for the current economic mess that we are in. There is much talk of regulation, codes of practice and of ethics, but very little by way of concrete recommendations on how to stop it all happening again. This is where corporate social responsibility, if practiced properly, can make a real difference.

Another reason for the increased public awareness of CSR is that CSR and sustainability reporting is on the increase. The *KPMG International Survey of Corporate Responsibility Reporting 2008** notes that, in that same year, "nearly 80% of the largest 250 companies worldwide issued [CSR] reports, up from 50% in 2005." This is a staggering increase over just three years, and reflects the way in which CSR has become a commonly-used, although often poorly-understood, business term. It is notable, however, that the companies producing the most substantial reports and glossy CSR brochures are large, mostly global firms. Small to medium-sized companies rarely have the time or resources to report on the same scale. For this reason, CSR is often mistaken for something that pertains primarily to multinational firms, rather than SMEs.

It is important to recognise, however, that even though smaller firms may not produce separate CSR reports, their relative silence on the issue should not be taken for a lack of engagement. As shown by the businesses profiled in Part II of this book, small firms are engaged in a wide range of activities that larger companies would describe as CSR. Good examples highlighted by the companies profiled in Part II include the responsible pricing and trading policies of Nova Partners (see **Case E**), the thoughtful consideration given to

---

*Available at http://www.kpmg.com/EU/en/Documents/KPMG_International_survey_Corporate_responsibility_Survey_Reporting_2008.pdf; last accessed 28 March 2012.

sourcing ethically-produced goods by Blackfield (**Case D**), or the informal but effective mentoring systems put in place by the Woodlands House Hotel (**Case G**). Though few of these smaller companies compile these initiatives into a separate CSR report to external stakeholders (for the reasons discussed in **Chapter 7**), their actions have real impact on the wider communities in which they operate.

There are many more SMEs than large firms in existence. In Ireland, for example, more people are currently employed by small and medium firms than by multinationals. The impact of responsible trading in the SME sector should not be understated, and the difference that can be made to society by engagement on the part of SMEs in CSR is very significant.

Despite the importance of the SME sector, much of the guidance available to businesses on CSR seems geared towards larger firms. The reporting standards and impact assessments all take time and resources. The examples of best practice most widely cited are generally from multinational firms, with which SMEs have relatively little in common. This all means that corporate social responsibility can be a particularly difficult area for smaller companies and organisations to understand and navigate. While this book is not exclusively focussed on SMEs, it does aim to address this gap, and provide a starting point for smaller firms to engage with the exciting and emerging business discipline of CSR.

The book is organised into two parts. **Part I** gives a comprehensive but concise overview of the field of CSR. **Chapter 1** defines the terminology used, and reaches a working definition of CSR which applies throughout the rest of the text. **Chapter 2** sets out the two main pillars on which CSR has been developed – the business rationale and ethical considerations, commonly referred to as the business and moral cases, respectively. **Chapter 3** sets out the history of CSR leading up to current trends in implementation, such as partnering with non-governmental organisations (NGOs), 'soft' codes of practice, etc. **Chapter 4** sets out a comprehensive list of the responsibilities that might be imputed to a company, and discusses in depth in each case what the motivations are, and where the line lies between CSR and altruism.

Chapters 5 and **6** deal with the increasingly complex web of standards in this area, and the importance of CSR reporting, including some interesting examples of innovative ways in which companies get their message across. Because of the importance of the SME sector as outlined above, and the relative paucity of resources available to smaller firms wishing to engage with CSR, **Chapter 7** focuses specifically on SMEs, considering what their responsibilities might be, and what help is available to them in engaging with this issue. Finally, Part I concludes with **Chapter 8**, speculating on some future trends in the area.

Part I is liberally illustrated by brief examples or illustrations, and also contains 17 separate, shaded 'exhibits', which detail particular aspects of CSR, highlighting best practice or describing particular initiatives. These combine to make a reader-friendly resource designed to cover the topics in a straightforward and accessible way.

So much for the theory; how does this translate into practice, particularly for smaller firms?

In **Part II**, senior executives of eight Irish businesses describe their own experiences in trying to run their businesses as responsibly as possible, and their understanding of what that means in their particular circumstances. A wide selection of indigenous firms was chosen from across the public and private sector, men and women, and north and south of the border. They range from a very new, two-person consulting partnership in Cork to a mining firm employing hundreds of people in Mozambique, but are mainly small firms, most of which have not formally begun to report on CSR, or to gather data about it within their own business. Despite this, we find that all of those interviewed have one or more projects or initiatives which, if their firm were larger, would be described as a CSR activity. It is fascinating to see how smaller firms in particular can be operating at levels close to best practice in key CSR areas, without the motivation of reporting externally on this good performance.

The stories told by these business leaders combine to form a sort of conversation, shedding light on what responsibility means to smaller firms. They speak not only of the 'what' – the difficulties they have faced, the particular learning experiences that have brought them to their current position, and where they see the future for their businesses – but also of the 'why' – what brought these initiatives or attitudes about, what difference this is making inside and outside the firm, and why it might make sense for others to learn from their experiences. In a sense, Part I presents the theory, while Part II is a snapshot of current practice. This voice of practice both illuminates and challenges the theoretical focus of the first part of the book.

Sheila Killian
Limerick
May 2012

Acknowledgements

This book would not have been possible without the assistance of the business people featured in Part II, whose generosity and openness in discussing their experiences of CSR have created a record that should inspire other firms grappling with the same issues.

The tremendous work of the editing team at Chartered Accountants Ireland Publishing must also be acknowledged – their patience and attention to detail show in the quality of the publication.

A special thank you to President Michael D. Higgins for his warm words of encouragement on the publication of this book; they mean a great deal.

Finally, the support of my colleagues at the University of Limerick, in particular the library staff, and the good humoured tolerance of my family have all made writing this book an interesting adventure.

Buíochas mór daoibh go léir.

Part 1

The Theory

Chapter 1

The Meaning of 'Corporate Social Responsibility'

As CSR is still emerging as a business discipline, it is understandable that the term 'corporate social responsibility' is open to many, differing interpretations. Lenssen *et al* (2007) describe corporate social responsibility as "a contested term", the meaning of which is not agreed. This chapter seeks to establish the boundaries of its meaning. Initially and most basically, we can look at each of the words in turn.

'Corporate'

'Corporate' is most commonly used in a legal sense to refer to incorporated bodies or companies: a corporate entity is one governed by the law of companies. However, CSR is a concept that is also embraced by many groups that are not incorporated, such as partnerships, charities, sports clubs, state bodies, trade unions, etc. Perhaps the dictionary definitions that are most helpful are:

"forming one body of many individuals; of or belonging to a corporation or group";[1] or

"shared by members of a group; joint".[2]

This sense of the word 'corporate' referring to a single body, from the Latin *corpus*, allows for the fact that *any* group or body can embrace the concept of CSR.

'Responsibility'

'Responsibility', in certain instances, can be taken to mean 'blame' – the person responsible for a wrongdoing, for instance, or the corporation responsible

---

[1] *Oxford Concise Dictionary*, 7th edition Oxford University Press, New York, 1982.

[2] *Chambers Pocket Dictionary*, Chambers Harrap Publishers Ltd, Edinburgh, 2001.

for some environmental disaster. There is also a sense in which responsibility is a burden, as when a person is weighed down by their responsibilities. However, the term 'responsible' can also mean 'mature' and 'ethical', and can equate to independence or the ability to work unsupervised or without regulation. A legal definition of 'responsible' refers to the inherent nature of the subject, and is "characterized by trustworthiness, integrity, and requisite abilities and resources".[3] The definition of 'responsible', therefore, covers blame and burden, but also maturity, an ethical approach and trustworthiness. CSR applies these definitions to business, suggesting that a firm, for example, can be held responsible for a higher standard of behaviour than that set down in hard law, perhaps an internal code. It also implies that a truly responsible business can be trusted, and so can operate without supervision in some areas.

'Social'

The word '*social*' can specifically refer to leisure rather than business activities, as in a 'social' occasion. It can also refer to social class, or socialism, but none of these meanings relate particularly to its use in 'corporate social responsibility'. More useful definitions include "pertaining to the life, welfare and relations of human beings in a community"; "pertaining to, devoted to, or characterized by friendly companionship or relations"; or "living or disposed to live in companionship with others or in a community, rather than in isolation".[4] This latter definition is also phrased in *Collins English Dictionary* as "living or preferring to live in a community rather than alone".[5] This is interesting, as it could suggest that the 'social' in CSR positions businesses as active participants in their wider communities, and acknowledges the fact that companies do not exist in isolation but are instead part of what Jensen and Meckling (1976) call "a nexus of contracts"[6] between a wide range of different stakeholders. In practical terms, this means that anything a business does – hiring, expanding, importing – will have a ripple effect on the surrounding community – not just the physical community defined by geography, but the community of similar businesses, suppliers, customers, shareholders and so on. If we think of the

---

[3]   Merriam-Webster's *Dictionary of Law*, Merriam-Webster US, 2000.

[4]   *Random House Dictionary*, Random House Reference, 2010.

[5]   *Collins English Dictionary*, 6th Ed (HarperCollins, 2003).

[6]   Jensen, M. and Meckling, W. (1976), "Theory of the Firm: Managerial Behavior, Agency Costs and Ownership Structure", *Journal of Financial Economics*, October, 1976, 3(4), 305–360.

firm as operating within a social system, it makes sense to consider the impact of its actions in this way.

EXHIBIT 1: STAKEHOLDERS

The term *'Stakeholders'*, as more fully explained in **Chapter 3**, is often used to describe the wide group of individuals and bodies that, in some sense, 'have a stake' in a particular organisation. As such, stakeholders include shareholders, employees, the local community, government bodies, suppliers, customers and special interest groups.

'Corporate Social Responsibility'

Analysis of the individual words will not, of course, lead to a full understanding of the concept of CSR. However, examining the constituent words 'corporate', 'social' and 'responsibility' above gives us the idea of a group or body (such as a company) that can be trusted, operating to higher standards than those demanded by external law, conscious of its impact on stakeholders and the wider community. This is a useful starting point.

The idea of CSR meaning something more than that required by law is an important one. Compliance with legal requirements is a very basic responsibility for any person or body. If the law demands, for example, that workers are paid a minimum wage, then an employer cannot claim that compliance with this rule is part of their CSR policy. However, often an employer, particularly if operating in a country in which there is no minimum wage specified in legislation, may lay down internal codes which exceed compliance with the law. Starbucks, for example, specifies in their Code of Conduct that "Wage and benefit levels should address the basic needs of workers and their families".[7] This idea of a 'living wage', regardless of whether or not a minimum is specified by law, is common among multinational firms operating in a range of different regulatory environments. Because it exceeds basic legal compliance, it forms part of their CSR strategy on labour. (More detail on this area is given in **Chapter 4.**)

---

[7] Starbucks Commitment: statement of beliefs. Available at: http://www.citinv.it/associazioni/CNMS/archivio/strategie/starbucks.html#star, last accessed 28 March 2012.

Some other key terms are used interchangeably with CSR, such as the 'triple bottom line', 'corporate citizenship', 'corporate responsibility' and, to an extent, 'sustainability'. Each of these terms and their relationship with CSR are briefly considered below.

The 'Triple Bottom Line'

This term dates to the publication in 1997 of *Cannibals with Forks: Triple Bottom Line of 21st Century Business* by John Elkington (Elkington, 1997). The book makes the case for businesses to take action in support of social as well as financial causes, and identifies three 'bottom lines' on which a business could report. These loosely equate to 'people', representing society and the wider stakeholder group (see **Exhibit 1** above), 'planet', representing the environment, and 'profit', representing the default reporting of financial performance to shareholders. The focus of triple bottom lines has been on reporting, rather than on strategy or goal-setting, under each heading. The idea was very influential in moving the debate about CSR forward, and normalising the idea of accountability in the social and economic spheres. It is not a reporting standard, however, and does not present a template for reporting. As such, it is an important concept, and one which can inform the strategy of a company, but not something readily applied to day-to-day business decisions.

Corporate Citizenship

This term first appeared in early 2000 on company reports[8] and commentary, and has its origin in the idea that since corporations can act as legal persons – own property, take court cases, be sued, etc. – then they should take on some of the responsibilities, as well as the rights, of citizens. It is a loose term, incorporating many aspects of responsibility, and links into the sort of identity-based values or ethics described in **Exhibit 2** below. The term is somewhat problematic, however, as corporations obviously do not hold all the rights that are afforded to real citizens – the right to vote, for example, or to hold a passport. The corollary of this is that corporations do

---

[8] Such as the *Volvo Environmental Report 2000*, which includes on page 5 the sentence "Volvo's reputation is founded largely on its history of corporate citizenship". Available online at http://www.volvogroup.com/SiteCollectionDocuments/Volvo%20AB/values/environment/env_report_2000_eng.pdf; last accessed 15th May 2012.

not have all the responsibilities that citizens do, such as those around compulsory military service, or education. Critics of the term dislike this imperfect mapping of the concept of citizenship onto the role of a corporation.

Corporate Responsibility

This term is essentially an abbreviation of CSR, with the conspicuous omission of the word 'social'. Critics wonder if it is more straightforward for a company to be considered simply responsible, than socially responsible? Could it be interpreted to simply mean compliance with government regulation, with perhaps a little fair trading thrown in? Others feel that 'corporate responsibility' is a more descriptive term, taking into account all aspects of the company's activities, and its impact on internal stakeholders, such as employees and investors, as well as the wider environment, sustainability, etc. Corporate social responsibility or CSR remains a more prominent term, however, and is used throughout this text.

Sustainability

'*Sustainability*' or '*sustainable development*' is a slightly different concept to CSR, but it is worth addressing here because many firms, in reporting their CSR activities, include them in a sustainability report. Like the triple bottom line, the term was popularised by Elkington (1997) to describe a way of doing business that did not erode the firm's relationship with the environment, or with society. So, for example, a logging firm which sought to be sustainable could replant trees to replace those it used in production. This would ensure that the production process itself was sustainable, and would be able to continue indefinitely without damaging the key source of value for the firm. This form of sustainability is good for both the environment and the business. If applied to *people,* the other non-financial pillar of the triple bottom line, sustainable development involves taking care of the relationship the firm has with, for example, local communities, to ensure their long-term support. Because it is applicable to both the environment and society, the idea of sustainability is part of CSR but, as we will see in **Chapter 3**, it does not cover all that is required in a broad-ranging CSR policy. Nevertheless, the terms are often used interchangeably, particular in company reports.

Practice

A review of some of the CSR reports from major multinational firms for 2011 shows that CSR is held to include the following ideas:

- Developing an ethos, set of values or way of operating that reflects the values of the leaders of the organisation. For example, *The Guardian* call their annual sustainability report, *"Living our Values"* and publish on their website a code of conduct also expressed in terms of values.[9]
- Contributing to the welfare of the community, which may be defined as the immediate hinterland of the business premises, or the wider or virtual community of potential customers or major suppliers. For example, Disney's CSR strategy, largely limited to employee volunteering and charitable donations, is geographically focussed: "The majority of our giving is concentrated in and around the cities of Orlando, Florida; Los Angeles and Anaheim, California and New York City, New York where the majorities of our employees live and work."[10]
- Running the business carefully and well, taking care not to harm any of the stakeholders or the environment. A good example of this approach is Google's informal slogan: "Don't be evil," as described by CEO Eric Schmidt in a *Newsweek* article in 2005.[11]
- Branding using CSR activities to contribute to the overall trust of the general public in the brand. A good example is The Body Shop, which built a major international brand by marketing the natural qualities of their products and the fact that they are ethically produced without testing on animals.
- Cause-related marketing. A good example of this, discussed later in **Chapter 3**, is the link between Ballygowan and breast cancer charities.
- Selecting hiring and/or sales practices that reflect the company's values and make a positive contribution to the community. For example, the US pharmacy chain Walgreens has an active policy of promoting the recruitment of people with disabilities.[12]

---

[9] See http://www.guardian.co.uk/info/our-values; last accessed 28 March 2012.

[10] See http://publicaffairs.disneyland.com/donation/; last accessed 28 March 2012.

[11] Schmidt and Varian (2005).

[12] See http://www.walgreens.com/topic/sr/disability_inclusion_home.jsp; last accessed 28 March 2012.

- Aspects of the modern corporation, including the relative power of companies and governments, which give rise to the need for firms to be responsible. (This is discussed in detail in Smith and Lenssen (2009). The basic idea is that with power comes responsibility, and furthermore, that when companies have great power, there is a corresponding need for them to acquire legitimacy, and be trusted by the communities around them and the customers who buy their products. See **Exhibit 15** in **Chapter 8** for a further discussion on trust.)
- Developing targeted initiatives that leverage the company's reach to help the public to donate to a particular cause. A good example here is Diageo's "Arthur's Day", which encourages customers to buy Guinness linked to a company donation to a charitable trust.
- Complying with voluntary standards of operation in key areas, such as waste management and the environment, labour and, particularly, the supply chain. This can be seen in the CSR reports of most multinational firms. The supply chain is an area of particular concern to retailers (as discussed in **Chapter Four**), due to the fact that, increasingly, major retail brands are being held responsible for the conditions in the third-party factories supplying them.

All of these aspects of corporate social responsibility will be explored in the coming chapters.

As noted by Wan-Jan (2006: 3): "Practitioners seem to be practising CSR despite the lack of a universally agreed definition." Nevertheless, it is useful at this stage to have a common idea of what we mean by CSR. In this book, CSR refers to the idea that *any* body of persons, which may include a business, should act within a wider society in a way that is ethical and accountable, and make business decisions by reference to the responsibilities that body of persons holds to a wide group of stakeholders, including shareholders and the environment. It is important to bear in mind that the definition is not static. We will see over the coming chapters that responsibilities change over time – what was perfectly acceptable in the past, for example, in the area of health and safety, may no longer even meet basic legal requirements.

As discussed in **Exhibit 16** in **Chapter 8**, an organisation's own understanding of its responsibilities should also change over time as it engages more with stakeholders and develops a more well-thought-out policy. For example, a firm may start by thinking of CSR as something extra that the firm does for social good, perhaps a charitable donation, or sponsorship of community-based events. However, corporate social responsibility is far more fundamental to the strategy of any business than the way in which it advertises, or the donations it makes to charity. As we will see throughout this book, CSR is about trading responsibly and well, building a sustainable business, providing a good service or product that is safe and useful, dealing responsibly with all the stakeholders of the firm, etc. Charity and sponsorship are like the tip of the iceberg that is CSR – the most visible part of the story, but perhaps the least significant. **Chapter 4** details the wide range of potential responsibilities that make up CSR, placing philanthropy in its appropriate context.

The following chapter describes the main rationales for embracing a CSR strategy, focussing in particular on the common ideas of there being both a business and a moral case to be made for a business to act in this way. Following this, we recap on the history of CSR, discussing how the responsibilities ascribed to companies have changed over time, before getting down to detail in **Chapter 4** on what the particular responsibilities of a business might be.

Chapter 2

The Business and Moral Arguments

Introduction

There are many reasons why organisations should begin to engage in CSR activities and formulate a CSR strategy. Proponents of CSR often group these reasons under the headings of 'the moral case' or 'the business case'. The former refers to choosing to take an action because it is 'the right thing to do'. So, for example, there is a strong moral case for avoiding child labour or forced labour in the production of goods sold. Slavery is regarded as a universal wrong and, so, goods produced using forced labour are widely regarded as tainted. A CSR initiative with a strong business case is one where the 'doing good' and 'good for business' sets clearly overlap.

For example, SABMiller is one of the world's biggest beer producers, operating in an industry that uses a great deal of water. Much of the production occurs in countries where clean water is at a premium, or in Southern Africa, where it is not available to all communities. In 2008, the company set itself the target of reducing its water consumption by 25% over the following seven years. In making the announcement, SABMiller CEO Graham Mackay said: "In an increasingly water constrained world it is critical that we become as efficient as possible, whilst working with communities to protect water resources. This is an extremely challenging, but achievable target, and sets a new industry benchmark."[13]

SABMiller's water-reduction target is clearly good for the environment, as well as for the communities near which it operates. It will almost certainly also save the company money in the long run, as the production process will be leaner, and water charges will be reduced. There is, therefore, a strong business case to be made for an initiative such as this.

---

[13] Press release from SABMiller, November 2008. Available online at http://www.sabmiller.com/index.asp?pageid=149&newsid=780; last accessed 28 March 2012.

The 'Moral Case'

For those approaching CSR from a moral perspective, the first principle is often a variation of the Hippocratic Oath: "First, do no wrong." In a business context, this means first – before considering anything else that could be done – the firm should avoid 'doing harm' in any sense to the environment, local communities, employees, etc. This involves decisions on *how business is done* on a day-to-day basis, rather than *what business can do* for stakeholders outside the firm. The moral case for CSR, 'doing the right thing', is generally based on some set of ethical values, even if these are not formally articulated. These values generally align with the values of the leader or founder of the business, or the ethical norms of the society in which the business operates. In **Part II** of this book, a series of Irish companies are profiled and, repeatedly, the rationale for engaging in CSR is given in these terms – i.e. the values with which the founder was brought up.

EXHIBIT 2: IDEAS ON BUSINESS ETHICS

Though corporate social responsibility, as we will see, involves far more than just ethical decision-making, ethics certainly form a key part of it. It is worth briefly considering some of the main approaches that have been applied to business ethics. Outlined below are the four main ethical approaches that are useful for business: deontological, utilitarianism, rights-based, and virtue-based.

Deontological Approach

A deontological approach is similar to that of most religions in that it emphasises an absolute moral code. A follower of the approach is expected to do her duty, regardless of the consequences. You can see aspects of the deontological approach in corporate codes of conduct – there are certain things, such as fraud or insider trading, that are simply prohibited, regardless of the consequences at the time. For example, in their wide-ranging World Bank study of corporate codes of conduct, Smith *et al* (2003) found that, in almost all cases, there was an absolute prohibition on the use of forced labour. Regardless of the circumstances or the scale of the practice, forced labour is almost universally regarded as unethical. It is simply wrong.

Utilitarianism

In contrast to the deontological approach, utilitarianism (a form of consequentialism) – sometimes called 'results-based ethics' – hinges on the idea that the morality of an action is completely determined by its consequences. If nobody is hurt, there is nothing wrong with the action. In many scenarios where a business or personal decision needs to be made, some people will be affected adversely, while others will be helped, depending on the choices made. A purely utilitarian approach involves weighing up the impact on all parties and choosing the course of action that minimises harm or maximises good.

In practice, as we go through life, we do not separately weigh the consequences of all of our actions one by one. Instead, we have developed a sort of shorthand that assesses the morality of an act according to the consequences that usually flow from actions of that kind. So, for instance, littering is generally regarded as wrong, because the damage done to the environment outweighs any good achieved. Thus, rather than separately evaluating the consequences each time an opportunity to litter arises, the simple guiding rule that littering is wrong will be internalised. This kind of shortcut approach is called 'rules-based consequentialism'. Stealing will generally be regarded as wrong because the harm done to the victim normally outweighs any moral good that is done by the theft. However, the rule is not absolute: in extreme circumstances, such as the theft of life-saving medicine from a wealthy vendor, stealing may not be regarded as wrong.

A business example of a utilitarian approach is the following goal in the Fairtrade Labelling Organisation International (FLO), Fair Trade International Code of Conduct Standards for Hired Labor (cited in Smith *et al*, 2003: 163): "After two years of certification, eliminate use of pesticide-impregnated plastic bags, unless demonstrated that production is impossible without the bags." The existence of the goal shows that the FLO judge that, as a rule, the use of pesticide-impregnated plastic bags is undesirable. However, the bad consequences for the environment of their use may be outweighed by the adverse consequence of banning them, if this means a loss of production.

Rights-based Approach

A rights-based approach does not reflect a specific moral code; rather it simply assumes that all people and organisations have certain minimum rights and, therefore, that a course of action should be chosen which, as far as possible, does not infringe those rights. So, for example, as in the case of GlaxoSmithKline in **Exhibit 12**, it would be considered fair for a company to sell a product more cheaply to a population that needed such a cheap sale in order to preserve their right to life while, at the same time, fighting a patent infringement in another area where those circumstances did not apply.

Virtue-based Approach

Finally, a virtue-based approach to ethics is based on Aristotle's ideas of how to be, rather than what to do. It is not based on rules, but rather demands that ethical decisions are approached by reference to the character or image that has been defined for the organisation. A decision on a particular situation could be reached by asking, "Am I the sort of person who would ...?" or, "Are we the sort of organisation that ..?" For this to be effective, obviously everyone in the organisation must be clearly aware of the sort of virtues or values that the firm as a whole espouses. Since they are not based on rules, they must be demonstrated by the leaders within the organisation. In a sense, as described by Audi (2009: 25), "Virtue ethics is indeed a kind of ethics of role-modelling."

Despite the fact that companies do not have personalities, the language of virtue-based ethics can act as a common currency in propagating corporate culture, and ensuring that all employees apply the same ideas of ethics to everyday situations. It is, however, quite individualistic, and dependent on the values of the leaders. In large firms, it can be somewhat unpredictable in application.

Virtue-based ethics can be effective if the firm is small, however, and where the leader projects a strong sense of personality on the organisation. In **Part II**, Mary Fitzgerald of the Woodlands House Hotel (Case G) speaks in virtue-based terms about the ethos of the business: "We grew our business around the delivery of an honest product... People see us as credible people."

Ethical issues can be complex, however, and ethical values are not universally recognized. For example, for some people, a business cannot be considered ethical if it makes profits from alcohol or gambling. For others, such activities would not present a problem, whereas experimentation on animals or the development of cluster bombs would not be morally acceptable. Nevertheless, basic universal principles of integrity, honesty and transparency are generally associated with responsible and ethical business.

The 'Business Case'

A different, though overlapping, set of rationales for implementing a CSR strategy within an organisation is referred to as the 'business case' for CSR. This is built on the premise that a business's obligations to other stakeholders are secondary to its role in making a profit for the shareholders. Having made that assumption, CSR initiatives or actions are evaluated on that single scale. Thus, if an initiative or approach can result in increasing a business's profits in one way or another, it is said to have a strong business rationale and, so, a business case can be made for adopting it. Most environmental initiatives have a strong business case, since they usually involve using less energy, packaging or transport, with resultant cost savings that increase profit.

The business and moral cases for CSR are often presented as though they were in opposition: either there is a strong business reason to take some action, or the firm is doing it in response to ethical concerns. For example, it is easier to create an instant business case for strategic positive initiatives than for the avoidance of negative behaviour. The sponsorship of a local charity event may bring in goodwill and, thus, can be justified in the marketing budget. However, re-engineering a production facility so as to reduce some inconspicuous but damaging pollution has less immediate upsides.

In fact, there is rarely a conflict between the business and the moral rationales, as long as one evaluates the benefits of taking or evading particular actions over the appropriate time-period, and taking into account all of the costs and benefits. For example, the use of forced labour, as noted in **Exhibit 2** above, is universally decried as a wrong. Taking an extreme non-ethical stance, an argument could be made that eschewing forced labour in favour of a paid workforce increases production costs and reduces profit. However, this is a very short-term view. In the longer-term, the damage done to the brand of a firm by the use of forced labour in its production has a cost. The flexibility and loyalty of a well-paid workforce has a benefit. These two factors alone will outweigh the absence of wages in a forced-labour situation, effectively making a strong business case for prohibiting forced labour in an organisation.

Commentators on CSR often criticise particular initiatives on the basis that they are undertaken for business motives rather than some form of corporate altruism. This is to miss the point. As long as some good is done, in the form of a preserved environment, better labour conditions, etc., the precise motivation of the firm is not very significant. As long as consistently responsible behaviour is the outcome, the motivation is not of primary importance.

Chapter 3

Some of the History behind 'CSR'

While corporate social responsibility might be a relatively new term, as a concept it is very old indeed. One could argue that, in Ireland, CSR dates back to the Brehon Laws, first documented in the Seventh Century, and in the oral tradition from hundreds of years earlier. As noted by Mary Dowling Daley in her book, *Irish Laws* (1989),[14] the Brehon Laws detailed when a business was and was not responsible for damages caused by the negligence of a trader. For example, modern property developers might be interested to learn that, if a visitor to a building site in ancient Ireland was injured, the liability of the builder depended on whether or not that person had legitimate business on the site. Furthermore, doctors were obliged to live near fresh, running water, and had personal liability for any wounds that failed to heal. Thus, the idea of traders, professionals or any form of business having responsibilities to those with whom they had a business relationship was well-established in ancient Ireland.

Basic concepts of corporate social responsibility can also be seen in the far more ancient Babylonian *Code of Hammurabi*.[15] Hammurabi was the king of Babylon from 1795 BC to 1750 BC. The laws he made were discovered in 1901, carved on a tall, black stone monument in the ancient city of Susa (now in modern Iran), and provide a unique insight into the rules applying to business almost four thousand years ago. Among the first written laws in the world, the *Code of Hammurabi* required businesses and trades to behave responsibly, and the laws were accompanied by brutal sanctions. Builders, for example, were required to build well and sustainably. If a newly-built house collapsed and killed its occupier, the builder would be put to death immediately.

In Japan also, ideas about business responsibility can be traced back to a time before there were incorporated companies. An early example is the

---

[14] Dowling Daley (1989).
[15] For a discussion on the Code of Hammurabi, see Claude Hermann Walter Johns' entry entitled "Babylonian Law – the Code of Hammurabi" in the 11th Edition of the *Encyclopaedia Britannica*, 1910–1911.

sanpo yoshi or 'three-way good' business principle of the 1600s.[16] This precursor to the modern concept of the triple bottom line (see **Chapter 1**) meant that any business transaction should be designed in such a way as to benefit the seller, the buyer and society at large. The *Omi Shonin* merchants from Honshu practised these principles which, in practical terms, meant that part of their profits was always invested for the benefit of the community in which they operated – for example, building bridges or schools. This philosophy had a direct economic benefit, making the merchants welcome as they expanded their businesses all over Japan. The international conglomerate, Marubeni, had its origins in this system.

In the UK, the origin of corporate social responsibility is generally dated to the Industrial Revolution, which transformed the old rural, feudal relationships and, for the first time, created an urban working class. In the early 1800s, as people migrated from the land to live near the new factories, welfare problems emerged around housing, health, child labour and the education of workers. Because of the sheer pressure of numbers in the city, however, the new industrial capitalists did not feel the same sense of responsibility towards their workers as had been shown by the rural landowners. The England portrayed by Charles Dickens was that of the survivalist employee, struggling from an early age with no economic safety net and very few rights. Blowfield and Murray (2008) describe how these poor conditions led to civil unrest within the cities.

Many of the later industrialists saw the root of this civil unrest not in terms of workers' rights or poor pay, but as the breakdown of the system that still applied in rural areas, where wealthy landlords cared for the tenants and workers on their estates. They chose to address the problem in an indirect way, by giving to charities serving social causes, or building schools or hospitals. This triggered a new era of philanthropy that marked the Victorian period, and involved a recognition by business that it had changed the fabric of society and should take some responsibility for this.

EXHIBIT 3: CADBURY – CHANGING THROUGH TIME

In 1909, the chocolate-maker Cadbury, firmly in the Quaker tradition, was a pioneer of responsible business and particularly known for valuing its labour force. Cadbury had established the village of Bournville to provide good housing within easy reach of its factory, with schools,

---

[16] See Poliszcuk and Sakashita (2010) for a more complete explanation.

shops and open spaces that were far ahead of their time. When the *London Evening Standard* reported that the company was aware of the widespread use of slaves on the cocoa plantations in São Tomé which produced some of its key raw material, the public was shocked.

The company sued for libel, but over the course of the trial, the head of the firm, Lord Cadbury, admitted that he knew slaves were used on the plantation, and furthermore, that he considered this essential for the profitability of the enterprise. The good name of the company was damaged, however, and they switched to a different supplier in Ghana, persuading several other chocolate producers to do the same. Today, the company's website explains the decision without reference to the court case, simply saying: "In the early 1900s, William Cadbury made the decision to source cocoa, a vital ingredient for our chocolate brands, from Ghana, then known as the Gold Coast. He left São Tomé where forced labour was being used to harvest cocoa."[17]

Almost a hundred years later, in 2000, the company, by then Cadbury Schweppes, was again accused of ignoring the fact that their cocoa was produced using forced labour, an issue highlighted in a BBC documentary.[18] This time the company reacted immediately by rejecting slavery outright. In the ensuing media storm, however, Cadbury was unable to prove that it was really aware of the conditions of workers on the plantations. Neither were many of the NGOs working in the area, but the public outrage was directed at Cadbury and other large chocolate producers.

The following year, in September 2001, a new protocol on eliminating child labour and forced labour in the cocoa industry was introduced. This Harkin–Engel Protocol[19] is congruent with the relevant International Labour Organisation (ILO) convention, and includes a six-step action plan for cocoa manufacturers aimed at eliminating forced labour. While it is not legally binding, it is supported by leading industry bodies, governments and human rights organisations, and is generally thought to have improved conditions in the industry.

---

[17] From http://collaboration.cadbury.com/ourresponsibilities/ethicaltrading/cocoa-sourcing/Pages/responsiblecocoafarming.aspx; last accessed October 2011.

[18] See Blowfield and Murray (2008) for a description of the two events.

[19] See http://www.cocoainitiative.org/images/stories/pdf/harkin%20engel%20protocol.pdf for details; last accessed 15 May 2012.

In both cases, Cadbury was tried in the court of public opinion and found wanting because of the working conditions in a separate company which supplied them with cocoa. In 1909, moving to a new supplier solved the PR problem for Cadbury. One hundred years later, however, a more thoughtful, industry-wide response was needed. This case neatly illustrates how much more is expected of companies as time goes on, and underlines the importance of knowing where your products come from and ensuring that your response to bad news is in line with current thinking.

The Modern Debate about CSR

In modern times, the first serious debate on CSR emerged in the 1950s and 1960s. In his essay from 1960, "Can Business Afford to Ignore Social Responsibilities?",[20] Keith Davis argued that social power flows from the taking on of social responsibilities, and that the exercise of these responsibilities is the price paid by business for social freedom. This proposal was debated through the 1960s, together with the ideas that a business might spend money on issues with no immediate obvious payback, and that CSR should incorporate these voluntary actions, i.e. those that go beyond what is required by law.

With all new ideas, there is generally a period of debate and competition before more widespread acceptance. The first major challenge to the CSR debate of the 1960s came from the American economist Milton Friedman in an essay in the *New York Times Magazine*. In the article, "The Social Responsibility of Business is to Increase its Profits",[21] Friedman argued that when a business engages in philanthropy, the managers are effectively stealing from the shareholders and trying to emulate the job of government. Friedman took issue with the rather woolly definitions of CSR that were pervasive at the time, and with the lack of rigour applied by other theorists attempting to define the responsibilities of business. In reducing the purpose of a business to a simple shareholder model, he brought clarity to the debate. His arguments were straightforward, and simple to understand. However, at the same time, he severely narrowed the focus of the discussion about CSR over the following years.

---

[20] Available in Cragg *et al* (2009).

[21] Friedman (1970).

In the 1980s, the debate took another step forward with the introduction of the idea that CSR should incorporate the primary economic duties to the shareholders and employees, as articulated by Friedman, *with* the wider ethical context and additional responsibilities to society at large. In 1984, Edward Freeman published his influential book, *Strategic Management: a Stakeholder Approach*,[22] and introduced the idea of stakeholders in a company, including, but not limited to, shareholders. Economic responsibilities were considered to be part of, rather than opposed to, a business's responsibilities to society at large. This simple idea rapidly took hold and forms the foundation for CSR as we now know it.

Peter Drucker took Freeman's ideas and incorporated them into the mainstream of business strategy. In his classic 1974 book, *Management*,[23] Drucker had categorised the responsibilities of business as first minimising the adverse impacts on society of the business in general and, secondly, seeking to engage in solving social problems only where there was a good business opportunity to be exploited in doing so. In 1986, however, he argued:[24]

"The proper social responsibility of business is to turn a social problem into economic opportunity and economic benefit, into productive capacity, into human competence, into well-paid jobs, and into wealth."

This was the birth of the 'doing well by doing good' movement which continued through the early 2000s, as exemplified by such popular business books as Kellie McElhaney's *Just Good Business: The Strategic Guide to Aligning Corporate Responsibility and Brand*.[25] The most widespread understanding of CSR at that time was that, as long as its principles could be completely aligned with the shareholder-value purpose of a firm, they had merit and, therefore, could be applied to the overall benefit of all of the stakeholders of a business. This represents a partial swing back towards the views of Friedman, in that it accentuates the primacy of shareholder value. It does not, however, limit itself to the narrowness of Friedman's argument, i.e. that the only purpose of a firm is to maximise profit.

Since the economic downturn, writing on CSR has again moved towards the wider stakeholder argument, fuelled in part by a general disillusion with the impact of serving shareholder value only. There is more and more work

---

[22] Freeman (1984).
[23] Drucker (1974).
[24] Drucker (1986: 62).
[25] McElhaney (2008).

being done on impact assessments, for example, and on a business's responsibilities for welfare in its supply chain. As the discipline of CSR matures, it is to be assumed that the pendulum of argument will swing in shorter arcs as thinking converges around what responsibilities are reasonable to attribute to business.

Trends in CSR Implementation

While academics argue about how far the responsibilities of a business extend, practitioners struggle with implementation. As demands on companies grow, driven both by the expectations of external stakeholders and the aspirations of internal leaders, there will inevitably be a drive to achieve things that are beyond the scope of what the company can do by itself. If, for example, a business feels that it carries a responsibility for the water quality of the community in which it operates, it will immediately face challenges, such as a lack of expertise in the area or, perhaps, a lack of credibility in the eyes of the local community. Very often, however, there are external bodies with which a business could usefully partner in order to achieve its CSR goals more efficiently.

Recently, the trend has been towards partnerships either with NGOs or with other companies in the same sector. NGOs often have the expertise to tackle a social issue, but lack the resources, whereas companies may be well-placed in terms of resources, but lack the knowledge and access to tackle such issues. Partnering can offer a useful solution.

A good example of partnering can be seen in **Part II** of this book, in the case of Kenmare Resources (see **Case B**, and also as mentioned in **Exhibit 4** below).

There are many charities with which a company can partner. The United Nations Children's Fund (UNICEF), for example, is well known for its work with children. In Europe, it mainly presents as a charity, and its interface with companies is commonly through seeking donations or corporate sponsorships for fundraising events. In common with other UN organisations, however, UNICEF increasingly recognises the pervasive influence of business on society, and its power to influence how people live. For this reason, it has launched a Corporate Engagement Initiative to work with companies who wish to leverage their work for the benefit of vulnerable children. Most of the engagement is still centred on fundraising, or cause-related marketing. A good Irish example is Aer Lingus, which organises collections among passengers for the fund. Since June 2009, UNICEF has also sought to act as a resource for companies of all sizes who wish to implement best practice in their business operations.

A related trend is the move to industry-wide initiatives. Rather than simply moving forward in a new business practice, a large organisation may choose to consult with its peers in an effort to establish new guidelines for the way in which the business is operated. A good example is the Kimberley Process[26] on diamonds. Following concern at the way in which diamonds were widely used to fund conflict, particularly in Africa, the UN passed a resolution in 2000 that brought companies, governments and civil society groups together to develop protocols aimed at establishing the provenance of rough diamonds. The Kimberley Process Certification Scheme (KPCS) now controls 99.8% of the international trade in rough diamonds, and allows them to be sold as "conflict-free". It has successfully restricted the trade in conflict diamonds in a way that no single-company initiative could have, and is an excellent example of how voluntary codes of practice can have very wide impact.

Such codes of practice are often described as 'soft law' because, being voluntary, they lack financial or legal penalties for non-compliance. However, to dismiss them as having 'no teeth' misses the point. They have far more reach than so-called 'hard law', as they impact on the global operations of companies. For example, the Kimberley Process has effected real change in the diamond industry. This is such an international market that no individual country could have achieved this level of change through their legal system. Because codes of conduct are drawn up with representatives from the affected industry, they tend to be workable, and so are widely implemented. Their primary contribution to CSR is in raising the bar of reasonable behaviour in a way that legislation could not, and in providing a benchmark for all firms in an industry to emulate best practice.

EXHIBIT 4: PARTNERING WITH NON-GOVERNMENTAL ORGANISATIONS (NGOs)

More and more companies are finding that, rather than taking on work directly in the communities in which they operate, it pays to partner with pre-existing charities, community groups or non-governmental organisations (NGOs), and facilitate them in doing work in areas where the company wants to help.

---

[26] See www.kimberleyprocess.com.

A good example of a successful pairing between a company and a charity is shown in **Part II, Case B**, in the case of Kenmare Resources. Kenmare operates a mine in a remote area of Mozambique. With a desire to address the healthcare issues of and improve medical care available to the community surrounding the mine, the company decided to partner with a Danish NGO with medical and dental expertise but not the resources to deliver the desired result. Both company and charity brought something to the table and, together, were able to achieve more than either one could manage on their own. Kenmare provided the financial and logistical support required and, together, they now provide healthcare and medical support to eight to 10 villages. Working with government-employed health staff, they provide training to community volunteers. The impact of the intervention by Kenmare on the wider community is far greater than it would be if it simply provided health services at the mine itself.

Not all partnerships work out so happily, however, and there can be pitfalls in partnering, for both the corporation and the charity. Not least among these is the challenge of managing the expectations on both sides. Charities may expect simple, no-strings attached donations, and be wary of being co-opted to sell the message of the company in the community. Companies may expect that their involvement with a charity will absolve them from integrating the shared values which are agreed between the NGO and the firm as applying to their joint initiative into their core business. The language used by the two groups and their preferred way of doing business can also lead to serious communication difficulties in terms of what exactly is being achieved. For example, when a company talks of consultation, it may mean giving the charity observer status at some board meetings. A charity may take the same term to mean having a real voice, having its concerns taken on board or even having a veto on certain operations. It is important, therefore, that terms of engagement are clearly set out and agreed at the beginning of the process.

The match also needs to be right in terms of mission: the NGO needs to be operating in the area in which the company wants to make progress, and the company needs to have the same approach as the

NGO to the communities or environment that might benefit from the work. Like so much in the area of CSR, the key seems to be leadership and sincerity. If this is something a company really wants to do, then it will be able to incorporate the sensitivities of the NGO. Likewise, the charity partner needs to be upfront about its concerns, and what it can and cannot deliver, rather than simply holding out for a maximum donation.

There is usually a power-imbalance between the two organisations, however. The company will generally be far larger and more influential than the NGO, so it is important that there is mutual respect in the relationship. At worst, a partnership can be seen as a fig leaf for the company, and can undermine the legitimacy of the NGO. At best, the two parties can educate each other in the process of working together, and between them deliver a good service to the particular set of stakeholders they are seeking to serve.

Some international NGOs provide useful resources to companies wishing to develop their CSR strategy. Two that offer expertise in best practice in the areas of the environment and human rights are CERES,[27] a coalition of investors and environmental groups working with businesses, and Amnesty International,[28] who have an extensive section on their website on economic, social and cultural rights.

The history of CSR described above with all its trends and counter-trends shows how CSR as a discipline is developing in an iterative manner, responding to changes in society. The field is still evolving rapidly, and significant differences remain in the level of compliance with CSR principles in different parts of the world. In South Africa, for example, the Stock Exchange pioneered a socially responsible index of companies, and the idea of businesses having a responsibility to the communities in which, or near which, they operate is now widely accepted. Environmental issues are less prioritised in South Africa than they are in the US, however. While the definitions of CSR are changing, so are the means by which companies set out to

---

[27] See www.ceres.org.
[28] See www.amnesty.org.

meet their CSR goals. Partnering with NGOs or across industries is now widely done and is an effective way of achieving more than a business could manage alone. Codes of Practice or 'soft law' are also widely applied to improve the standard of practice among companies. All of these factors raise the bar in terms of how businesses operate and meet their responsibilities, and the next chapter looks in more detail at what those responsibilities might comprise.

Chapter 4

What are the Responsibilities of a Business?

The possible range of responsibilities that might apply to a business under 'corporate social responsibility' is vast. However, in general, the main areas include:

1. economic responsibilities;
2. environmental responsibilities;
3. responsibilities to the local community;
4. responsibilities to employees and human rights;
5. governance responsibilities – preventing corruption;
6. product safety and quality;
7. responsibilities for the supply chain; and
8. endorsement or support of particular causes.

Each of these responsibilities is dealt with in turn in this chapter, and both the business and moral cases are discussed. **Chapter 5** will then look at the practical guidance available on how best practice can be implemented and reported in each area.

Figure 4.1 below presents a 'mind map', which is a simple visual representation of the various responsibilities highlighted in this chapter. These are the main areas covered by CSR standards. The mindmap is intended to give a single-page overview, and can also be used to quickly assess the breadth of a company's CSR engagement.

1. Economic Responsibilities

A primary (economic) responsibility of any business is to make a profit. Indeed, as mentioned in **Chapter 3**, Milton Friedman[29] was of the view that this was a business's *only* responsibility. Clearly, a business needs profit in order to continue in operation and to provide a return for shareholders. Without profit, there is no job security for employees, no continuity for

---

[29] Friedman (1970).

Figure 4.1　**Responsibilities of a Business**

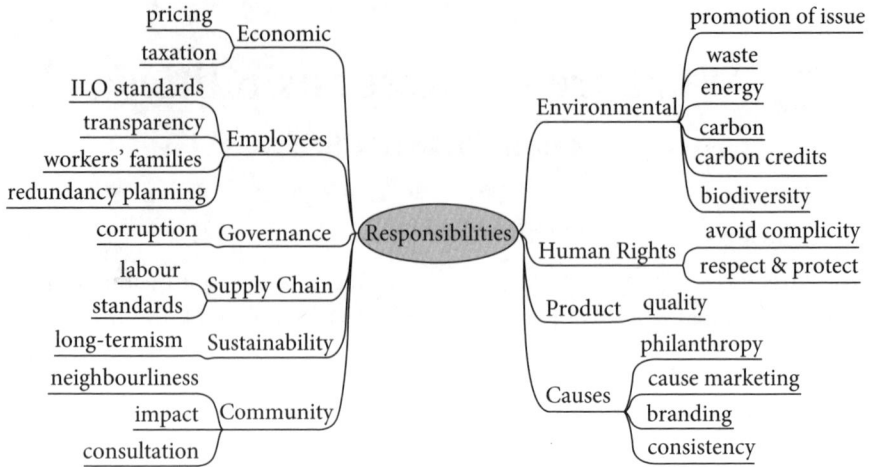

customers or suppliers, no tax for the government, etc. Economic responsibilities extend beyond profit, however.

The economic responsibilities of a business as understood in the context of CSR are to make a profit in an ethical and sustainable way, with minimal negative impact on society or the environment. Each business decision needs to be taken in this light. This means that a business that understands its economic responsibilities will have careful guidelines for every aspect of the way in which it operates. These guidelines will cover, for example, the way in which it deals with suppliers, employees, customers etc. For example, while it is natural to negotiate the best possible terms, a responsible business will be conscious of not putting undue pressure on suppliers, at least not to the level at which they are put at risk. This is particularly important in times of recession. Similarly, the terms offered to customers should be fair, and pricing should be clear and comprehensible.

EXHIBIT 5: PRICING RESPONSIBLY

The idea of responsible marketing is gaining traction with the public and within industries. Responsible marketing means more than clear and transparent pricing. It also covers the way in which a business sells, particularly to vulnerable groups. So, for example, it includes issues such as marketing to children; marketing complex products such as medicines, credit or loans; the use of falsified claims in advertising; stealth marketing; insider trading at auctions, and so forth.

Then again, what if a company finds itself locked into a way of selling that could be considered unethical, but is simply the norm in the industry? For example, Don Flow runs Flow Automotive,[30] a chain of over 30 car dealerships in the US. As in many parts of the world, a certain amount of haggling is normal in buying a new or used car; a price is named and the customer negotiates. Flow Automotive analysed their own sales, and found that the people who typically paid most for their cars were those on the lowest incomes, who had limited negotiating skills. As reported in Erisman (2004),[31] Don Flow felt this amounted to "taking advantage of the least able". He introduced a new form of very transparent pricing. The strategy benefited the company as well as the customer, reducing the overhead associated with a prolonged negotiation process, and winning a niche market with high customer loyalty.

A further example can be seen in the case of Nova Partners, a Human Resources and training consultancy profiled in **Part II**. Nova prioritises really transparent pricing, which is not the norm in their industry. This has a short-term cost in that it does not allow them to charge more to those who can afford to pay more. In the medium term, however, it is likely to pay dividends in terms of their reputation, and in their market share among smaller clients.

Tax avoidance and evasion are one aspect of economic responsibility that is getting more attention in recent years (see **Exhibit 6**). In some ways, this is the most basic aspect of corporate citizenship, and no business that evades its tax can be considered responsible.

Fair competition also comes under the general heading of economic responsibilities. All businesses compete, but responsible businesses do not engage in unfair competition, enter covert cartels or seek to take advantage of a monopoly position. Furthermore, economic responsibilities also encompass fair dealing with suppliers. For example, when the US clothing firm Patagonia[32] places orders to its manufacturing suppliers in developing countries, it is careful to give as much notice as possible of the order, so as not to drive the supplier into using overtime unnecessarily. This is because the buyers at Patagonia know that overtime is likely to put pressure on the

---

[30] See www.flowauto.com.

[31] Erisman (2004).

[32] See www.patagonia.com.

labour standards operated by the suppliers, and may lead to breaches of the labour code. In taking this care with suppliers, it not only builds a better relationship, but also offers Patagonia more assurance that their clothes are not produced in sweatshop conditions.

EXHIBIT 6: TAXATION

Tax is not the first thing that comes to the mind of most business owners when considering the topic of CSR. Yet, when one thinks about it, paying one's fair share of tax is really the most basic level of responsibility a business has to the society in which it operates. The big question is: what constitutes a fair share? Most companies engage tax consultants at one level or another, and these consultants often earn their fee by ensuring that the business pays as little tax as possible. In fact, it is not uncommon for the fee to be couched in those terms – a saving compared to the tax that would have been paid in the absence of the consultation. This can be verified by a simple online search for the phrase 'save tax', which returns the websites of thousands of tax advisors.

The moral case for a responsible approach to taxation is clear: businesses consume government resources, and so have a moral obligation to pay their fair share of taxes. This is particularly true in a time of recession, when a company's contribution to the exchequer can result in a more stable society, better educated workforce, better infrastructure, etc. Increasingly, a responsible approach to taxation is not only seen as the right thing to do, but as a part of risk management. Adopting a very aggressive approach to tax planning puts a business at risk of incurring costs and penalties following a successful challenge from the taxing authorities. Compliance can also protect the reputation of a firm at a time when tax evasion has led to street protests targeted at major corporations.

With regard to tax, CSR demands more from businesses than staying on the right side of the law in terms of its tax planning. It means, literally, being responsible and reasonable in terms of taxation. Thus, engaging an accountant to advise on compliance is good; getting advice on how to arrange one's affairs so as to minimise the overall tax bill is generally considered reasonable; but aggressive and artificial tax schemes are moving deep into the realm of irresponsibility.

From a business perspective, many of the economic responsibilities of CSR more or less justify themselves. From a moral point of view, they are justified by the ideas of sustainability and fairness in dealing with business partners. So, certain categories of CSR activity are more or less uncontested. Other economic responsibilities, however, do not directly contribute to the bottom line of the business, and so the rationale for a business acting in a responsible way may be less obvious. The operation of informal pricing cartels, for example, or the demanding of 'hello money' from new suppliers, are the kind of activities that, while clearly reprehensible, will deliver short-term profit, even if at the cost of long term reputation. A coherent CSR policy that embraces an organisation's vision of sustainability will always take a long-term view. A good example is the Blackfield Clothing and Surf School, as featured in **Part II (Case D)** of this book, who see the fair payment of tax as part of their responsibility as a business, particularly in times of recession.

2. Environmental Responsibilities

The environmental aspect of CSR is perhaps the most widely understood, at least in Europe and North America. The debate about global warming, for example, has made us more conscious of our impact on the environment and, at the same time, businesses are subject to a raft of new legislation and guidelines on pollution, recycling and other environmental issues.

Typical environmental issues within CSR include minimising packaging, waste and energy usage, as well as sourcing materials and goods for sale close to the point of manufacture or sale so as to minimise associated carbon costs. It is reasonably clear that a responsible firm will aim to minimise pollution – this is simply part of being a good neighbour and minimising the negative impact of the business on the environment. The idea of minimising the carbon footprint of both employees and goods is also gaining ground, as companies seek to cut down on unnecessary travel and shipping costs. For example, many organisations have expanded their use of teleconferencing to address this issue. In doing so, they are reducing their impact on the environment, making their products or services inherently 'greener', and also saving the costs associated with travel and shipping.

Exhibit 7: Carbon Credits

An organisation may want to reduce its carbon credits because of a belief that this is better for the world, since carbon contributes to climate change, or simply because it wants to cultivate a greener image or work towards carbon-neutrality so as to market its products or services as being environmentally sound. Carbon credits or carbon offsets for companies are, in essence, a simple idea. Basically, any activity which produces carbon can be balanced by another which reduces carbon, such as the planting of trees or the promotion of alternative energy.

If you are concerned about the carbon footprint of your business on an on-going basis, or about the carbon cost of travel, for example, associated with a special event such as a conference, you can use the services of a carbon credit company. They will calculate the carbon cost, and calculate what would be needed on a global basis to balance this impact. They can then sell you the appropriate carbon credit.

There are a range of such companies, the best of which are non-profit (such as Offsetcarbonfootprint.org), which sell carbon credits to companies enabling them to offset the carbon cost of their production. The funds are used to invest in carbon-positive projects, generally in developing countries, such as forestry, projects that prevent deforestation, or renewable energy projects. These projects can have a very positive impact on local communities.

While it is attractive to claim carbon-neutrality through the purchase of credits, there are hazards in this approach. There is rising scepticism among commentators about the value of many of the projects undertaken in the developing world, particularly hinging on concerns about biodiversity, inappropriate forestation and projects undertaken without consultation with local people. There is also a wider unease about the fact that most purchasers of carbon credits are in developed countries, while most of the carbon-reducing projects are not. This contributes to a sense that businesses in developed countries are effectively buying a licence to pollute, backed up by the needs of developing countries. Finally, there is the concern that the purchase of credits ultimately allows those who can afford carbon credits to continue to produce goods in an unsustainable way, thereby increasing their competitive advantage over smaller, and perhaps more sustainable enterprises.

In order to avoid these criticisms, companies considering the use of carbon credits should regard it as an interim measure rather than as the sole means by which they work towards carbon neutrality. They should carefully check the credentials of the credit seller, and ensure that their projects adhere to the guidelines of international bodies such as the International Emissions Trading Association (IETA), the International Forest Carbon Association (IFCA), or the Climate, Community & Biodiversity Alliance (CCB). In this way, companies can have more assurance that the money they pay for carbon credits is working well. Carbon credits, when used, are generally reported on the company website or in the sustainability report. This makes them a highly visible first step for companies and can lead to greater awareness across the business of the carbon cost of travel or shipping. This can be very useful in effecting a paradigm shift within the business.

Some businesses actively promote environmental issues through their marketing or through promotional material on their premises. For example, conspicuously using recycled materials, or asking hotel customers to reduce their use of fresh towels is a way of getting the message across that the business is committed to preserving the environment. Tollymore National Outdoor Centre, as profiled in **Part II (Case G)**, personifies this commitment in their very beautiful and very *green* building. The building itself is a sort of headline statement of the commitment of the centre to sustainability and to the environment. It is underpinned, however, with a series of simple but persistent steps taken to reduce Tollymore's environmental impact. Simple things, such as adjusting the timing on heating systems, or ensuring that computer terminals are powered down at night, underpin the overall commitment Tollymore has to the environment, and ensure that this commitment permeates all of their business activities.

Such a commitment has meant a substantial up-front cost, however. The cost of building the Tollymore centre was particularly high because of the high specifications used, but the running costs are far lower than average. In addition, the building makes a spectacular statement about the values of the centre which, it is hoped, will bring rewards in the future.

Finally, businesses that promote the fact that they take steps to manage their impact on the environment also need to consider the way in which they are sourcing their products and raw materials, and the impact this has on communities. This can sometimes lead to a conflict. For example, the use of palm oil to make sustainable fuels has been controversial at times, because some palm oil plantations have been poorly managed, and have contributed to deforestation, monoculture and food poverty in the countries in which they operate. Neste Oil[33] is a large Finnish oil company whose move into the production of sustainable fuels has led to it being listed in the top 100 sustainable companies worldwide.[34] Despite this reputation, in 2011, the firm was forced to respond to international criticism of its operating practices by explaining that it uses only certified palm oil and tries, as far as possible, to use waste products and by-products in making its fuel.[35]

Most initiatives in the area of environmental sustainability have both a business and a moral basis. Cutting down on waste, packaging, travel, shipping and energy will save money as well as the planet, while marketing the idea of the company as a responsible firm that uses recycled materials and identifies with green issues will increase market share and enhance the reputation of the business. For example, an article in *The Green Hotelier*[36] quotes David Jerome, senior vice-president of corporate social responsibility at InterContinental Hotels Group (IHG) as follows:

"We know from our in-depth consumer research that corporate responsibility influences buying decisions. A recent survey of 6,000 of our Priority Club Rewards members highlighted that 38% of our guests choose hotels based on their environmental credentials."

Avoiding disastrous spills and hazards makes obvious business sense, as well as fulfilling the moral responsibility to nearby communities. Carbon offsets are generally well-supported by business rationales that centre on the value of marketing and branding the firm as a green company. The example of Neste Oil shows the importance of looking down the supply chain at the impact of the manufacturing process, or of monoculture in the production of important raw materials. This also certainly makes sense for a business that

---

[33] http://www.nesteoil.com.

[34] See http://www.global100.org/annual-lists.html, where Neste Oil is listed at number 19 for 2012; last accessed 15 May 2012.

[35] See the company's response to the Public Eye Award nomination at http://www.nesteoil.com/default.asp?path=1,41,540,1259,1260,16746,16748; last accessed 15 May 2012.

[36] *The Green Hotelier*, Issue 52, Do customers care? – The green market is resilient, September 2010. Available online at http://www.greenhotelier.org/index.php?option=com_content&view=article&id=194%3Aissue-52-do-customers-care&Itemid=27&limitstart=2#content; last accessed 15 May 2012.

is seeking a global reputation as a sustainable operation. All in all, environmental issues are well supported by both business and moral arguments.

3. Responsibilities to the Local Community

While most firms accept that they have a responsibility to the community in which they operate, it is not always clear what they mean by the term 'community'. For some, it is the community of their employees and their families. For others, it may be the local people who live within a short range of the business premises. In general, the idea that a business has community responsibilities is very well understood in Europe. Small businesses, in particular, see themselves as an integral part of their communities, and the idea of sponsoring the local football team, golf classic or community centre is a very natural one. Such sponsorship can be part outreach and philanthropy, and part advertising.

However, beyond this basic level of giving, there are more fundamental aspects to being part of a community. Most of the companies profiled in **Part II** who have Irish operations identify strongly with the locality in which they operate. David O'Mahony of O'Mahony's Bookshop (see **Case C**), for example, speaks with considerable pride about the business's long connection with the history of Limerick, and articulates a sense of responsibility that he feels all local businesses share for the image and welfare of the city.

It can be helpful to think of an organisation's responsibilities to the community in terms of neighbourliness. A good neighbour does not cause noise issues, impact on water rights, endanger the local ecosystem or the health of local residents. So, as well as thinking about the obvious benefits a business can bring to an area, such as employment, spin-off trade to local businesses, and perhaps a welcome flow of people into depopulated rural areas, CSR demands that consideration be given to the impact of locating a business in a particular area. This can be difficult as, in most cases, a new business will bring changes to an area that might not be universally welcomed; for example, the visual impact of the business premises, noise pollution during construction, increased traffic and congestion, new people, changes in the affordability of local housing, etc. Thus, a factory or business run by a responsible firm will do more than just sponsor local teams, give to local charities, or support the fundraising efforts of local schools. It will also take steps to mitigate the adverse impact it is having on the community or area in which it operates.

Any hostility felt towards a new business will usually be eased when the business engages with the community on a level more profound than sponsorship. The most useful initiatives are linked to what a business does and what it can uniquely do in an area. So, for example, a computer company might endow a local school with IT infrastructure, or link up with the career guidance function to mentor students. **Part II** of this book is full of good examples of this. O'Mahony's Bookshop (**Case C**) takes an active part in helping local writers to find a market for their books; Tollymore National Outdoor Centre (**Case G**)hosts free information sessions for the local community on aspects of the outdoors; and Blackfield Surf School uses its educational remit to have the children they teach clean the beach on which they learn.

These are all positive things, which are relatively easy to put in place, and which have a solid impact on the communities that benefit from them. Firms establishing a new branch or outlet need to be sure, however, that they are not simply replicating strategies which were effective in other areas. A genuine consultation with local people can go a long way towards ensuring that the firm minimises its negative impact, and is well-accepted in a new community. If a business makes an effort to work with local people to see how their concerns can be addressed, preserves local amenities as far as is possible, and respects the rights that were enjoyed before the business came to the area, they will largely avoid serious conflict and create a better standard of living for all of their employees.

Kenmare Resources (profiled in **Part II, Case B**) is a good example of this approach in action. The company operates a large mine in what was previously a very undeveloped part of Mozambique. From the beginning, it was aware of the potential negative impact the mine's presence might have on the area, and it worked with local community leaders to address their most pressing concerns. Today, the company continues to work with the community, and rather than simply keeping locals informed, it maintains a genuine, two-way dialogue with them. To achieve this, Kenmare established a Development Association, which is under the joint control of the company and the local people, and which sets priorities for civic engagement. The Association holds bi-monthly meetings at which the company and members of the community discuss issues of importance to them. In this way, Kenmare is seeking to operate as part of the community rather than as something outside of it, looking in.

Like environmental engagement, the moral case for contributing to the community is clear and centred on the idea of neighbourliness, and minimising the adverse impact of a business. On the other hand, the business case for contributing to the community should be built around four main strategic advantages that accrue to firms with good community engagement:

1. Community Outreach

Community outreach is a way of marketing a business or organisation to its local community which, in turn, can provide it with customers, employees or services. It raises the profile of a new business, and makes those who have benefited from sponsorship, etc., more positively disposed towards giving their business to the firm, or choosing to work there.

2. Reputation

A good reputation locally can prevent prolonged local disputes, which can impact the national or international reputation of a firm. There are lessons to be learned from the example of firms that have been tied up in long, drawn-out local battles on environmental or safety issues. Many mining and oil companies, for instance, had their global reputation damaged by local disputes. A good example is Royal Dutch Shell, whose image was tarnished by its interaction with the Ogoni people of Nigeria.

3. Community-based CSR Initiatives

More generally, community-based CSR initiatives can create social capital for a firm. 'Social capital' refers to a wide range of intangible assets that are held within the people working in or living around a particular company. In the context of CSR, social capital is that level of acceptance of a business in the community which generates what is sometimes called a 'licence to operate'. This refers to the informal, unwritten permission granted by a community to a firm, an implicit tolerance for some level of inconvenience or loss of amenity in return for respect and support from the business.

4. Philanthropy

Finally, the philanthropy of a business can help to solve social problems in the immediate hinterland which, in turn, will make for a better environment in which to do business. For example, Kenmare Resources' work to improve local healthcare services as discussed in **Part II** (**Case B**), addresses an important need in the community. It also improves the welfare of the local population so that they are better able to engage in the life of the community, to run businesses that supply food and services to the mine, and to generally contribute to the life of the area.

EXHIBIT 8: BUSINESS IN THE COMMUNITY IRELAND (BITCI)

Business in the Community is a member-based organisation operating in both the UK (BITC)[37] and Ireland (BITCI)[38] that aims to help businesses become responsible and sustainable. BITC was founded in 1982 and has over 850 business members across Great Britain and Northern Ireland. The organisation is a charity, and works with businesses to help them engage in community projects. (They have moved away from the terminology of CSR, preferring to use the term 'responsible business'.)

BITCI was founded in the Republic of Ireland in 2000, with the blessing and support of the UK organisation. Its focus is on larger and multinational firms, and it has just over 60 members. Like its UK equivalent, it is a registered charity. (BITCI uses the term 'corporate responsibility' rather than CSR.)

Both of the organisations have comprehensive websites, which are well worth exploring. In particular, the UK site has a set of case studies and an excellent jargon-buster explaining in clear and simple terms what lies behind the language of CSR. The BITCI site also has a series of best practice examples, and they organise a very successful conference each year in late autumn. They have recently launched a certification standard called the Business Working Responsibly Mark, currently only open to companies in Ireland with over 250 employees.

The positive initiatives of community engagement described above, such as sponsorships, grants, prizes and so on, are easily justifiable in economic terms with a business case. When these initiatives involve employee action in fundraising for local charities, or devoting days to working on community projects, the external benefits to the firm can include better relations locally, while internally, better motivation and morale are often the result. Avoiding a negative impact is equally important, but can cost more and take more thought. For example, if waste is to be treated above the minimum standards, or water sources are to be shared, this may mean real financial expenditure, which needs to be balanced against the long-term, less tangible

---

[37] See www.bitc.org.uk.
[38] See www.bitc.ie.

value of good local relations. Increasingly, we see examples of firms that ascribe value to the intangible, and weigh in on the side of long-term, sustainable modes of operation. See, for example, the case of Interface Carpets at **Exhibit 17** below.

4. Responsibilities to Employees, and Human Rights

The area of employment and employee rights is perhaps the most regulated area of CSR and, so, because it is so heavily regulated, many business owners do not initially consider CSR to have a part to play in this area. Businesses operating within the EU are required to comply with a wide range of laws and regulations around equality, diversity, working age, job security, health and safety and minimum wage, all of which are contentious issues in other parts of the world. So, while complying with this raft of legislation is a minimum requirement, what is left for a responsible business to do in order to distinguish itself with regard to employee rights?

At its most basic, a business's responsibility to its employees is to implement the law fully in all aspects of recruitment, non-discrimination, pay, conditions, promotion and training. The next layer of responsibilities comprises those that are not covered by legislation. For example, legislation on minimum wage levels and maximum working hours is valuable, but responsible companies can take proactive action in this regard by increasing the transparency around planning for working hours and the allocation of unpopular shifts. This can demonstrate fairness, make it easier for employees to plan and lead to a more motivated and happy workforce. Recognition of a union or other kinds of employee representative groups is not required in all countries, although it is recommended internationally by the International Labour Organisation (ILO).[39] The ILO is a Turin-based agency of the United Nations, concerned with basic standards in the areas of labour internationally. While they do not have a direct focus on CSR, they operate a helpdesk[40]

---

[39] The ILO is an incredibly rich resource for businesses concerned about labour and employee issues. The organisation's standards set out best practice on a wide range of issues, and consulting them is particularly useful to firms operating in a country with whose norms they are unfamiliar. A full list of current ILO standards is available at www.ilo.org/global/standards; last accessed 4 April 2012.

[40] Details on the helpdesk are available at http://www.ilo.org/empent/areas/business-helpdesk/lang--en/index.htm; last accessed 4 April 2012.

for businesses, which addresses questions on such issues as minimum working age or hours of work. While these questions are not so troubling for companies operating solely within the EU, answers from the ILO can empower European companies to ensure that their supply-chain companies are not in breach of best practice.

ILO guidelines also go further than the law of many EU member states in the area of discrimination and equality. For example, Irish law prohibits discrimination on nine grounds: age, disability, gender, marital status, family status, sexual orientation, ethnic origin, religion and membership of the Travelling Community. The International ILO standard includes two further grounds: political beliefs and social origin, defined as including social class, socio-occupational category and caste. It is suggested that a responsible business will take care to operate to the higher ILO standard, and avoid discrimination on either of these two grounds.

Another key area of responsibility towards employees is that of training and mentoring. This includes providing opportunities to employees to progress their careers and acquire formal skills and qualifications. It also means the softer elements of on-the-job training and mentoring, which make for an efficient workforce and minimal industrial relations problems. It is striking how many of the businesses profiled in **Part II** of this book single out the people who work for them as the biggest focus of their CSR efforts. In particular, Mary Fitzgerald of Woodlands House Hotel (**Case G**) is very strong on the value of mentoring, and Brendan Salmon of KPS Colourprint (**Case A**) has created an exemplary open relationship with his staff.

In some countries, particularly where there is minimal social welfare, it is common for a business to formally take on some responsibility for the welfare of workers' families. A South African mining company may provide housing, for instance, or build a school. In Europe, the approach tends to be less formalised. For instance, if health insurance is offered as a perk to employees, it is common to allow it to be extended to their immediate families. It is also common to try to put in place a family-friendly environment, with some flexibility where it is needed. These policies are rarely gathered together and considered to be part of the firm's CSR strategy. Nevertheless, collectively, they can make a big impact on the families of employees. It is preferable to record and report these initiatives so as to preserve them, and so that the business can reap the reputational benefits of its responsible practices.

Finally, in these difficult economic times, organisations need to consider what CSR means when dealing with redundancies, should the need arise. The key here is openness, fairness and, where possible, providing an opportunity for those being made redundant to acquire new skills. In general, government agencies and local universities are happy to work with employees who are being laid off to help them acquire the skills they need to seek new work. A reasonable period of notice, a respectful way of delivering the bad news and a sincere effort to find new opportunities for those who are losing their jobs all go a long way.

The moral case for respecting employees' rights and creating a safe and fair working environment is perhaps best summarised by a quote from Mr Justice Peter Kelly in his judgment in the *Zoe Developments* case (1997): "You are entitled to make profits on the sweat of your workers, but you are not entitled to make profit on the blood and lives of your workers."[41]

Initiatives around employee rights are also popular with proponents of the business case. The business advantages of a well-motivated workforce with high morale are obvious: greater efficiency, reduced industrial relations problems and absenteeism, fewer accidents at work, more innovation and improved customer relations. So, how can CSR improve employee morale? There are two main ways. First, good working conditions, fair recruitment practices and family-friendly policies will contribute to a sense of fairness and belonging. Secondly, the involvement of employees in outreach and community-related philanthropy is an obvious way to contribute to a sense of pride at work, as well as helping with team-building.

Exhibit 9: Business and Human Rights

The core text on human rights is the Universal Declaration of Human Rights (UDHR),[42] drawn up after World War II and endorsed by most governments worldwide in the form of international treaties and law, general agreed principles, regional agreements and domestic law. Its 30 articles assert the right of all people to life, education, and fair access to law and healthcare, etc. The protection of these rights is generally seen as the job of governments. So, where does business come in?

The UN Global Compact has held that businesses have two obligations in this area. First, they should support and respect the protection of internationally recognised human rights and, secondly, they should ensure that

---

[41] As reported by Kerrigan (2006).
[42] See www.un.org/en/documents/udhr/; last accessed 5 April 2012.

they themselves are not complicit in human rights abuses. Areas that are emerging as being of particular concern to multinational firms, as shown by discussions at international CSR conferences, etc., include equality and diversity in the workplace, child labour and child access to education, water rights, community consultation and corruption. It is important for any business to be aware of these issues, and to review their own activities to ensure they are implementing best practice.

As noted in **Chapter 2**, it is easier to create a business case for strategic, positive initiatives than for the avoidance of negative behaviour. To sponsor a local team, for example, can be cheaper and more effective than advertising and, so, it is straightforward to justify this on economic grounds. Paying a fair wage that may be higher than the minimum, having codes and programs around dignity, respect and diversity, actively seeking to combat bullying, and providing a good level of benefits and family-friendly conditions, however, all cost money. Yet, it is striking that when many of the small firms profiled in **Part II** consider what CSR means to them, they focus particularly on the people they employ, and the way in which they try to build good relationships with and between them.

There is an excellent business case to be made for a loyal workforce. However, the benefits go beyond this. A really good working environment, where the leader is respected and listened to, is not only more pleasant to work in, as noted by Brendan Salmon in **Part II (Case A)**, but also makes it easier to foster the ethos of the company in all employees. In turn, this leads to far better customer relationships, and reduced risk of one or two employees letting down the reputation of the firm. A business with ambitions to be seen as responsible will see the advantages of spending time and money in this area.

5. Governance Responsibilities – Combating Corruption

Mention corruption to most business-owners, and they will immediately think of distant countries with warmer climates and more colourful flags. Overt bribery is relatively rare in most European countries, although many have lived through enough tribunals and investigations to shatter the myth that it is something which only happens far away. However, there are more organised and subtle forms of corruption than a brown envelope filled with cash, and it is on these that a modern European business needs to focus.

There is a great deal of regulation around bribery and political corruption. However, to those who seek to bend the rules, new regulation only poses a challenge, not a barrier. Indirect bribes can take the form of contributions to the pet causes of the target of the corruption, or the appointment of their associates to boards. This carries a double hazard: not only can it be a way of giving a covert reward, but it also dilutes the important role of boards of directors in overseeing the companies.

This area of corporate responsibility also covers forms of extortion embedded in trading practices: the most obvious and notorious may be the 'hello money' demanded from suppliers in the past by some large retail chains. Because this limits the ability of smaller firms to place their products on the shelves of supermarkets, it is clearly an anti-competitive practice which interferes in the free flow of good products. In some industries, it is common for suppliers to provide gifts to the people who are making purchasing decisions. This can be as innocuous as a Christmas bottle of wine, but it could extend to lavish training or team-building opportunities, provided, for example, by drug companies to doctors. The keyword here is 'appropriate' – if the scale of the gift is excessive, the motivation is naturally suspect. Finally, a business needs to be sure that its own marketing efforts cannot be construed as bribery. Well-intentioned gimmicks or draws can backfire badly if they are interpreted as an attempt to corrupt.

The moral case is clear on corruption and governance, and centres on accountability, honesty and maintaining the structures of the society in which the business operates. The business case can be made in four ways. First, what may initially present as a one-off bribe or corrupt practice can quickly become embedded into business practice. If this happens, then this petty corruption can represent a business cost for years to come. A variable percentage of turnover ear-marked for 'person or persons unknown' is obviously not something that most people want to have in their budgets.

Secondly, if a firm's culture tolerates corruption externally, it will be very difficult to outlaw internal corruption. If it's acceptable to hide or re-categorise company cash flows in order to facilitate bribery, then it is probably also acceptable to be less than transparent on remuneration, expense claims, the outsourcing of business to associates, etc. Once corruption is mandated, however covertly, it can become endemic within a firm, making internal governance very difficult.

Thirdly, a company that has influence over its peers needs to consider the kind of society in which it wants to operate. Corrupt practices damage the very business structures on which a business depends, undermining access to and certainty of law, the free movement of goods, planning, security, transparent public charges, etc., and creating instability.

Finally, there is the potential for massive reputational damage if a firm is found to have engaged in corrupt practice. While the risk of discovery might seem slight, history shows that, eventually, light is shone on dark practices, with consequent reputational damage for the people found to be involved.

Yesterday's business practices are no longer acceptable today. The logical extension of this is that practices that are ethically questionable but considered normal today are unlikely to pass future public scrutiny. If a particular business practice feels questionable by today's standards, it is not just possible, but likely, that one day it will be illegal and will carry sanctions. The best way to future-proof a company's reputation, then, is to act in a manner above the current standard. Outlawing all forms of corruption is an obvious place to start.

EXHIBIT 10: TRANSPARENCY INTERNATIONAL

Transparency International[43] is an organisation that addresses issues of corruption worldwide. It is perhaps best known for producing an annual Corruption Perceptions Index, which ranks countries according to the level of public sector corruption that is perceived there. While this is a useful tool in drawing attention to the seriousness of the issue of corruption, the organisation is often criticised for focussing on the places that have already been corrupted rather than on the root of the corruption, which include the actions of bribing companies. Furthermore, the Index has been criticized for focussing solely on corruption in the public rather than the private sector, and for ignoring the impact of tax havens and secrecy jurisdictions in facilitating corruption.

These concerns have been partly addressed by Transparency International in their newer index, the Bribe Payers Index, which assesses the likelihood of companies from a particular country to pay a bribe. It is more limited in scope, extending only to 28 countries, but it is interesting to see that the correlation between 'most likely to bribe' and 'perceived as most corrupt' is not perfect. The organisation also produces a wide range of reports and policy documents, and campaigns on the issue of corruption, targeting both governments and businesses.

---

[43] See www.transparency.org for further information; last accessed 5 April 2012.

6. Product Safety and Quality

Basic product safety and quality is a legal requirement. This is largely covered by consumer legislation, though it is worth noting that the standards vary widely around the world. There may be a legal requirement for clarity of labelling, age-appropriateness, the safety of products as they might reasonably be used and their fitness for purpose and appropriateness for the target market. Product safety is a relatively straightforward area in which the moral and business cases overlap substantially. Nobody wants to sell a product that may harm the consumer, even if the motivation is simply to stay in business and avoid being sued.

A compliant firm will observe the law. A firm that seeks to be socially responsible will go a little further. So, a responsible firm will aim to produce durable products, for example, to avoid the sort of built-in obsolescence that characterises some high-tech product ranges, and to make their products affordable to the target market. A good example can be seen in the case of Carambola Ltd, profiled in **Part II (Case H)**. Colm describes how, in choosing what to include in school lunches, the company first considers the nutritional value of the food and, only if they are satisfied at that point, move on to think about the pricing, etc. This has led them to supplying juice rather than water, despite the fact that there is a greater cost involved. The company is striving to deliver more than the minimum requirement in terms of product, and this will have a long-term impact on their reputation.

7. Responsibilities for the Supply Chain

This is perhaps the most contentious area of CSR, particularly for small firms. The basic idea is that companies are responsible for issues arising not only in their own business, but also in their suppliers. So, a car with components made using child labour, or an outsourced function with poor labour standards, can be held to be the responsibility of the seller or marketer of the main brand. If a retailer is selling a product that turns out to be produced in dangerous or illegal conditions, this can be very damaging for their reputation. At the same time, if the retailer is small, it can be challenging to patrol their supply chain, and be sure of the provenance of all the goods being sold. In the last few years, however, several high-profile firms have suffered reputational damage because of the actions of their suppliers, and the ensuing scandals have brought this issue very much to the forefront of the public consciousness. As such, it merits careful attention from business owners and managers.

A recent example, documented in Frost and Burnett (2007) is that of the very poor working conditions in Foxconn, the large Chinese company to which the manufacture of iPhones was outsourced by Apple. Shocking pictures emerged in 2010 of nets that Foxconn had erected to prevent suicides by employees jumping from the roof. Apple suffered a massive backlash of bad publicity. In this case, the actions of the supplier had a definite impact on the reputation of the main brand. Interestingly, Foxconn also produces phones for a host of other brands, including Motorola and Nokia. However, it was Apple that suffered the backlash, since they were the largest customer, and because there was such marked contrast between the conditions in Foxconn and the public image of Apple. This case also shows the hazards of claiming a very high moral ground in CSR which is not fully backed up by practice. Beckett (2012) lists other brands using Foxconn to manufacture their products in their factories, which employ up to 1.2 million people in China. Nevertheless, most reports of poor conditions in Foxconn in the US describe the company as the producer of the Apple iPod or iPad. This may be because of the effect described by Jiao et al (2012) whereby firms with a high-profile image, whether derived from CSR or otherwise, are more vulnerable to the reporting of negative corporate events in the media. The fact that Apple is so strongly associated with Foxconn now means that most reporting of poor conditions at Foxconn will reflect on Apple, effectively giving the other brands which use Foxconn a free pass.

The question arises, however, as to how far back along the supply chain can or should a company have responsibility? In some industries, a really complex web of producers and wholesalers makes tracing products back to source a challenge. This makes it difficult to be sure that the goods being sold are ethically produced. Smaller firms face particular barriers in attempting to police their supply chains, as they may not have enough influence to demand adequate information. On the other hand, smaller firms are less likely to be held responsible for the actions or inactions of their suppliers, as shown above by the Apple–Foxconn controversy. In 2011, I put this question to the International Labour Organisation. They replied that the best recommended practice is for a firm to carry responsibility as far up the supply chain as it has a reasonable level of influence. This means making a genuine effort to choose suppliers in which a firm has faith, and to influence their suppliers to set higher standards in terms of human rights and labour rights, in so far as it is possible.

Even where a business decides to take responsibility for its supply chain, it is not easy, in practical terms. If you run a retail outlet and want to stock goods that have been produced in an environmentally friendly or sustainable way, how do you know for sure that the choices you make will be the best ones? Should you, for example, choose organically-produced vegetables, even if these are flown half-way around the world to reach your shelves? How do you choose between organic and 'fair trade'? A good example of a firm making the most reasonable effort possible is given by Gerry Brannigan of Blackfield Clothing and Surf School in **Part II (Case D)**:

"We look carefully at what we sell … but there is a balance … Maybe instead of buying organic cotton, we might choose producers that are using dyes that may be approved as less damaging. Like everything else, it's a diminishing effect rather than a zero effect."

Clearly, Blackfield is actively trying to find the best products they can carry in the market in which they operate. They tried stocking organic cotton, but found that there was no demand for it on the island where they sell. Rather than simply giving up the idea of selling sustainable goods, they chose a compromise product, one produced more cheaply than a pure organic product, but still more eco-friendly than a standard garment.

Not only traders, but also consumers who are trying to shop in an ethical way are presented with what can be a baffling array of choices. Taking just one product as an example, coffee may be marketed as being 'fair trade', 'organic', 'affiliated to the rainforest alliance', 'songbird friendly', etc. These accreditations, in turn, can mean anything from a fair price for small producers of a key raw material, to farm practices that preserve local wildlife. Some certifications are clearly more rigorous than others. The Fairtrade mark, for example, is part of an international movement, and is a highly-respected indicator of a fair price being paid to producers.[44] If a product carries the SA8000 certification,[45] a standard issued by Social Accountability International, the human rights and labour

---

[44] See http://www.fairtrade.net; last accessed 5 April 2012.

[45] See www.sa-intl.org: SA8000 "is an auditable certification standard based on international workplace norms of International Labour Organisation (ILO) conventions, the Universal Declaration of Human Rights and the UN Convention on the Rights of the Child. This standard is the benchmark against which companies and factories measure their performance. Those seeking to comply with SA8000® have adopted policies and procedures that protect the basic human rights of workers." www.iioc.org/social-accountability-sa8000.

conditions around its production have been audited externally. These are so-called 'soft codes', similar to the Kimberley Process for diamonds described above. As such, compliance with these codes is voluntary, but they are of real value in the supply chain area. (The range of certifying bodies and the standards available are discussed further in **Chapter 5**.)

The business case for active and responsible supply chain management, like so many other areas of CSR, depends on taking a medium or long-term view of the business. Looking down the supply chain to detect questionable practices in suppliers can be expensive. If the business focus is short-term, then traders will focus on buying reasonably good-quality goods or components as cheaply as possible, and selling them at a profit. The provenance of the goods can be very much a secondary consideration. In the longer term, however, engaging with suppliers can help a business in a number of ways. It will insulate it against scandals and shocks in the event of child labour or poor working practices coming to light; it will give owners and managers more comfort as to the reliability and continuity of their suppliers, reducing the overall risk in this area; and, finally, it will allow a business – if it honestly reports the efforts it's making – to enhance its reputation or seek out a niche market for ethically-sourced goods.

A good example of this in Ireland is the food industry, where traceability is becoming the norm. Irish-sourced food is sought out by consumers, and customers are often willing to pay a premium for organic or fair-trade produce. In the Woodlands House Hotel case profiled in **Part II (Case G)**, Mary Fitzgerald discusses how they have used this to their advantage by continuing to use the best of local ingredients in their kitchens, and by giving details to guests on the source, charging a premium where necessary.

It can be difficult for a business to decide what products to stock, components to use, or where to outsource services. The key is to take decisions based on the idea of the business being sustainable into the future. What worked for Cadbury in 1909 would have been an inadequate response to their problems in 2000. If a firm is making a genuine effort to influence its suppliers to source well-made products that are produced in a fair way and with minimal environmental damage, then they are unlikely to run into a storm of adverse publicity in the near future. Taking the trouble to choose certified goods, or seeking a certification for key products, can provide some additional assurance. This is a rapidly changing area, and business leaders need to keep an eye on what is happening in their industry and the actions being taken by their peers.

8. Taking Responsibility for a Cause, and Cause Marketing

Many firms' CSR efforts are strongly associated with a particular charitable cause. In so far as this is pure philanthropy – the endorsement of a charitable or social cause – it is not unlike the first CSR efforts of the Industrial Revolution, described in **Chapter 3**. Philanthropy has an obvious moral imperative – doing good because one can – but the business case is more challenging to make. It can, in fact, fall at the first hurdle, echoing the arguments of Friedman in 1970 that charitable donations are a form of theft from shareholders. However, most firms have a strategy around the causes that they endorse, and use their support of charities to enhance their brand or to gain wider acceptance in the local community. A business will generally choose a cause because it is in some way congruent with its main brand, or relevant to its target market, and the endorsement of the cause will be used in advertising and marketing. This is not pure philanthropy then, but rather what is known as 'cause marketing' – the use of a charitable cause to sell a product or service (see the example of Pinkwashing at **Exhibit 11** below). Some of the most successful examples of aligning CSR efforts with a cause, as we will see below, lie in the middle ground between cause marketing and pure philanthropy.

At its most basic level, charitable giving can be a form of advertising that is particularly targeted at the local community. The advantages of having your business's name on the local teenagers' football jerseys are reasonably obvious: you are placing your brand at the heart of a local football game, where the viewers have a strong emotional connection to the team. In addition, having the reputation of supporting local charities can soften the image of a business and buy it social capital, as described in **Section 3** above. This can be achieved with less targeted donations. In small towns, banks, for example, or large supermarkets, are known for routinely supporting a wide range of charities with small donations – a prize in a table quiz, for instance, or support for a parents' school fundraiser. On the surface, there may seem to be no strategic choice, no single cause that is favoured. In reality, a scattergun approach can give a business a reputation as an all-round good citizen, always willing to support the community in whatever it does. These donations make the business part of the community, and give the sense that the firm is 'pitching in' in some way to meet the common goals of the local population.

EXHIBIT 11: PINKWASHING

You could be forgiven for thinking that ribbons for causes have been around forever – red for Aids, white for peace, pink for breast cancer. In fact, they're relatively recent, dating back to 1991 when the first Red Ribbon Project for Aids awareness was founded in New York. The pink ribbon for breast cancer started off when the Susan G. Komen Breast Cancer Foundation handed out pink ribbons to runners in its New York City race in 1991. It really only got national and international traction, however, the following year, when Estée Lauder, in collaboration with *Self* magazine, handed out a staggering 1.5 million pink ribbons at its make-up counters in the US.

At that time, the use of CSR-based and cause-related marketing was a rising issue in US business. Other brands rushed in to adopt the pink ribbon idea. In 1993, the cosmetics company Avon raised $10 million through the sale of pink-ribbon brooches and lapel pins. Within three years, the ribbon adorned everything from credit cards to clothing and, in December 1996, the *New York Times* described breast cancer as "this year's hot charity".

There is, however, a rising tide of cynicism against the use of the pink ribbon in branding. Part of this is due to the use of money raised. Sometimes, information on mammograms or self-examination is included with the ribbon, or a donation per item is made to a cancer-related charity. Increasingly, however, the ribbon is not associated with a donation to any breast cancer charity, but is simply designed to raise awareness of breast cancer by its presence on a product. This means that, essentially, all a company has to do is put the ribbon on its product, without making any donation to charity. Research coming from international consulting firms, such as McKinsey[46] or Cone Communications,[47] finds that, all other things being equal, consumers will choose a product that has a good cause visibly attached to the brand. Critically, the research also shows that if there is a good cause logo, buyers won't necessarily discriminate between those companies that contribute cash to cause-related charities or organisations and those that simply raise

---

[46] See http://www.mckinsey.com/insights.

[47] See www.coneinc.com/content1188.

awareness. The ribbon on the box will help to sell the product, at no cost to the producer. While it is always useful to raise awareness on health issues, pink ribbons are now so pervasive that the social good in attaching one to another product is questionable. As such, their widespread use where not attached to a cash donation, seems cynical.

The second common objection to the use of the pink breast cancer ribbon is more focussed, and targets the use of the pink ribbon by companies whose products can increase the risk of cancer. For instance, in 2008, the ribbon was adopted by Ford to sell its Mustang model in the US. Sulik (2010) describes how the disconnect between the macho image of the Mustang model and the cause of breast cancer awareness was too great in the public's mind, and the fact that car emissions can contribute to cancer was highlighted by people also protesting Ford's contemporaneous decision to cut health insurance for some of its workers. The company was accused of 'Pinkwashing' – using breast cancer to sell a product that, because of its emission levels, actually contributes to the incidence of the disease. The Breast Cancer Action charity in the US launched a 'Think before you Pink' campaign,[48] targeting the adoption of the breast cancer cause by inappropriate companies.

In Ireland, perhaps the best known company to use the pink ribbon for marketing is Ballygowan, who promote special pink-labelled bottles of water with a percentage of the sales price going directly to the cause. This works well, particularly as women are a significant part of the target market for bottled water, a donation is made to charity, and water is seen as an inherently healthy drink. There may be challenges to be overcome in the future, however, as concern rises about the safety of plastic bottles for drinking water, as documented by Posnik *et al* (2002).

The message for businesses from the Pinkwashing backlash is that cause-related marketing needs to be sincere, congruent with the brand and image of the company, and be consistent with the company's other activities. If the breast cancer cause genuinely gels with a company and its brand, then it can be a very successful and useful way for the company to both make a contribution to society, and boost its own brand image in the process.

---

[48] See http://thinkbeforeyoupink.org/; last accessed 5 April 2012.

On a larger scale, targeted philanthropy enhances the value of a brand. The key is choosing a cause associated with the activities and image of the firm, and one that is in line with the firm's overall culture and philosophy. The public can be cynical about businesses supporting charities, and the connection needs to be real, and to fit with the philosophy of the firm.

A successful example of philanthropy is the US link-up between Whirlpool and Habitat for Humanity. Whirlpool sells large electric appliances, such as refrigerators, cookers and washing machines. Habitat for Humanity is a non-profit organisation that builds simple, affordable housing for people in need. In 1999, Whirlpool began working with Habitat, announcing that it would donate a refrigerator and cooker to every Habitat home built in North America. The donations make sense – Whirlpool gives something that is needed by the charity, and which they can provide at a low cost, and their products become linked in the public mind with the idea of making a home for a family. The collaboration was so successful that, in 2005, Whirlpool announced an extension to their involvement with the project, and the company now supports every Habitat house built worldwide with appliance donations or financial sponsorship. The company also built a coalition of other large firms, such as Valspar Paints, and some of their retail distributors to work with Habitat. The key thing is that the connection between what the company does to make money (in this case, selling kitchen equipment) and the nature of the donation (facilitating the provision of homes to those in need) was clear and visible. Unlike the case of the Ford Mustang and breast cancer awareness, it is a credible and workable arrangement, which benefits both the cause and the marketing of the company.

Strategic links across an entire industry can be very useful, and can enable firms to achieve more in terms of supporting a cause than they could do by acting alone. For example, Airlink is an initiative of the airline industry group ISTAT, which organises cheap transport for NGOs bringing development aid to countries in crisis.[49] The airlines involved are giving something that only they can give – spare airline capacity – and at a far lower cost than could be achieved by other groups. By coming together, the airlines can achieve a better match for their CSR efforts, and make their giving go further.

---

[49]   See http://www.istat-airlink.org.

Conclusion

The range of responsibilities that a company can take on as part of its CSR strategy is vast, but most of them have a very sound business rationale. A firm that engages actively in fulfilling its economic and environmental responsibilities, as discussed above, will generally benefit directly in terms of profit, through reduced energy costs or better working relationships. Similarly, working well with the local community has reasonably immediate benefits in terms of social capital and acceptance. Endorsing causes and using them in strategic marketing can also increase sales, as will having safe, good quality and fairly-labelled products. On the other hand, operating to best practice standards with employees, paying attention to human rights and to better governance, and taking on responsibility for the supply chain can be costly initially, and have a less immediate impact on the bottom line of a business. However, apart from any ethically-based wish to do the right thing, a firm should consider the reputational damage it risks by not paying attention to these areas. A single incident can ruin years of careful work on brand image.

In many ways, acting in a responsible way can be more or less a matter of avoiding short-termism. If a business truly aims to maintain its relationships with key players both within and without the business over the long term, then a sustainable way of thinking should permeate decisions. No sensible entrepreneur would take a quick profit at the cost of a key relationship that may form the basis of future business. In the same way, taking the responsible action as a default leads to a more sustainable, long-term way of doing business.

Chapter 5

Standards and Regulation

As discussed in earlier chapters, CSR is commonly understood to be more than just legal compliance; it involves going a little further than what is required by regulation. Under each of the main headings in **Chapter 4**, it was outlined how best practice involves thinking as a neighbour, considering the impact of the firm on all of those who may interact with it or with its products. This is what it means to be responsible. One challenge, then, is in finding a way to benchmark with good practice, and ensure that a firm really is operating to the highest standards that are feasible. The law exists as an external benchmark for basic compliance. CSR standards were developed to fulfil a similar role for voluntary responsible behaviour – they provide a benchmark of best practice against which an organisation's actions can be measured. This chapter discusses the standards that are currently available, while **Chapter 6** will focus on reporting, once a standard has been chosen.

A wide range of such international voluntary codes and standards has been produced over recent decades. Some have been written by consulting firms as a way of promoting their own accreditation services, while others have more global buy-in, and were developed through a process of discussion involving companies, civil society and government. It can be challenging for companies, particularly smaller ones, to decide which standards to use. Sometimes these standards are categorized by reference to their level of *traction*, i.e. to what extent they are globally implemented or pervasive in a particular industry, and to their level of *sanction*, meaning the extent to which they are sufficiently standard in format to provide a real test of company performance. The easiest way to understand this is to compare standards.

In the production of coffee, Fairtrade (as discussed in **Chapter 4**), has high sanction as it is a standardised badge with a definite meaning to consumers. You can be sure that a product labelled as Fairtrade complies with certain minimum standards in terms of the price paid to the producers. 'Songbird Friendly', on the other hand, refers to coffee which is grown in the shade of larger trees, and so provides a habitat for birds. There is no external accrediting body, and no minimum standard that should apply. As a label, therefore, it has low sanction. In a completely different field, accounting standards, for example, have a high level of traction in that they are used widely, and also a high level of sanction in that they are demanding, and facilitate comparisons between companies. In CSR as in accounting, the best standards should score highly on both scales.

The United Nations Global Compact

The United Nations offers a range of resources to firms seeking excellence in their CSR practice. One of the most respected standards, and perhaps the first with real international reach, is the UN Global Compact,[50] which sets out 10 principles by which organisations should operate. The UN Global Compact is derived from the Universal Declaration of Human Rights, the International Labour Organisation's Declaration on Fundamental Principles and Rights at Work, the Rio Declaration on Environment and Development, and the United Nations Convention Against Corruption. It is generally regarded as the 'gospel' of CSR, with over 8,000 participants, including more than 6,000 businesses in over 100 countries. A business participant is expected to uphold and promote the 10 principles of the Compact (see below), report regularly on progress and pay an annual charge, ranging from US$500 for companies with a turnover of less than US$25 million to US$10,000 for very large companies.

The UN prescribes no set template for describing how the firm adheres to the Compact, but companies will commonly include a statement on their website or other such documentation stating that they have incorporated the principles of the Global Compact into the way in which they do business, or stating that they are guided by the principles. For example, Japanese electronics firm Olympus lists the principles on its website, and adds:

> "The principles of the Global Compact are incorporated into our Corporate Conduct Charter and Code of Conduct and reflected in our business activities. Through the interaction and reciprocal influence with other Global Compact participants, Olympus continues to practise these 10 GC principles in its business activities."[51]

---

[50] See www.unglobalcompact.org; last accessed 10 April 2012.

[51] See http://www.olympus-global.com/en/corc/csr/olycsr/philosophy/globalcompact/; last accessed 10 April 2012.

The principles of the UN Global Compact can be summarised as follows:

- Businesses should support and respect the protection of internationally proclaimed human rights and make sure that they are not complicit in human rights abuses.
- Businesses should uphold the freedom of association and the effective recognition of the right to collective bargaining, the elimination of all forms of forced and compulsory labour, the effective abolition of child labour, and the elimination of discrimination in respect of employment and occupation.
- Businesses should support a precautionary approach to environmental challenges, undertake initiatives to promote greater environmental responsibility, and encourage the development and diffusion of environmentally friendly technologies.
- Businesses should work against corruption in all its forms, including extortion and bribery.

While these may seem most applicable to global (or, at least, multinational) firms, a growing number of SMEs particularly in the UK are signing up to the Compact. For example, Tudor Rose is a small UK publishing company with 45 employees. Their website is badged with the Global Compact logo, and the words: "Tudor Rose is a full participant and signatory to the UN Global Compact, the world's largest corporate citizenship and sustainability initiative."[52] This is a relatively straightforward way for smaller companies to start their journey towards developing a full CSR policy.

As previously discussed, some of the international bodies linked to the UN, such as the ILO or Unicef, also offer a direct resource to businesses seeking to engage in CSR. They can be consulted directly, and also offer guidelines and other resources on their websites, such as information on best practice, or minimum standards to be observed.

The Global Reporting Initiative

The Global Reporting Initiative[53] (GRI) is a very large, non-profit, network-based organisation, headquartered in Amsterdam, with regional offices on all continents. It has brought together a wide range of stakeholders to produce a framework for the production of CSR reports, comprising frequently-updated

---

[52] See www.tudor-rose.co.uk.
[53] http://www.globalreporting.org; last accessed 10 April 2012.

sustainability and social responsibility guidelines, which companies can apply to their own businesses in a flexible and incremental way. Because of the detailed templates GRI provides to help companies produce a standardised description of how they are implementing CSR in all areas of their business activities, it is more widely applied by businesses as a reporting standard than the United Nations Global Compact. As well as helping with the actual report, however, GRI is useful in benchmarking, as most of the information needed to produce reports is freely available on its website.

EXHIBIT 12: CHANGING STANDARDS GEOGRAPHICALLY

The Cadbury case presented in **Exhibit 3** is a good illustration of how CSR standards have changed through time, not only in terms of how companies are expected to behave, but also in terms of how we expect them to react to public pressure. Unfortunately, this positive evolution of CSR standards does not apply evenly across the world. The high standards of health and safety or employee care that are enjoyed in Europe, for example, do not apply globally. Even now, children are working in gold mines in Peru with very little protection under the law. Health and safety standards in many parts of the world would seem abysmal by EU standards. Worker protection, freedom of assembly, fair living wages and basic leave entitlements simply do not exist for many workers.

For a European company that has expanded outside of its home country, particularly to a developing country, this issue can present a serious challenge to its CSR strategy. If you have a strong vision of the sort of firm you want to be, and how your corporate social responsibility can serve that mission, how do you respond to operating in a country with dramatically lower wages and longer working hours? How do you deal with the thorny question of child labour? On the one hand, is it fair for you to pay workers in Europe far more than you are paying their colleagues in a sister company in, for example, Indonesia? On the other hand, if you pay European wages in Indonesia, you will be pricing yourself far above the market in terms of salaries.

The best objective guidance for such work-related issues comes from the standards developed by the International Labour Organisation, as mentioned in **Chapter 4.** These standards do not aim for uniformity; rather they recognise the different conditions that apply in different parts of the world. They aim for what they call 'decent work', meaning the ability to earn a 'living wage', with workers enjoying basic rights and social protection. For instance, the standard on wages does not set out a minimum hourly rate of pay, but rather proposes wages that reflect the ability to earn a decent living, are paid regularly and in cash, with no limitations on how they can be spent.

The standard on child labour sets out a range of minimum ages for particular kinds of work, depending on the number of hours to be worked, access to education and the location of the work. These standards allow any business expanding into an area with which it is not familiar to quickly establish what the best recommended practice for their line of business is. This is a real help to companies seeking to behave responsibly, and is a vast improvement over simply benchmarking off other companies.

Sometimes, a single company will operate different standards in different geographical locations because of outside pressure. For example, in 1998, GlaxoSmithKline (GSK) was involved in two patent lawsuits. One was against a Canadian firm that sought to manufacture a generic version of GSK's anti-depressant, Paxil. The other was against the South African government, naming Nelson Mandela as a defendant, who sought to distribute generic anti-retroviral drugs used in the treatment of HIV/Aids. Following a worldwide campaign on the latter case, GSK agreed to make their own, patented anti-retroviral drug available very cheaply in Southern Africa and other Southern countries. Nevertheless, GSK continued to fight the Paxil case in Canada. As reported by Craig Smith (2003: 14), the CEO, Jean-Paul Garnier, explained:

> "Some months ago ... I said that I did not want to be head of a company that caters only to the rich. I made access to medicines in poorer countries a priority and I take this opportunity to renew that pledge. We have 110,000 people who go to work every morning because they are pro-public health. We have to make a profit for our shareholders but the primary objective of any policy put forward in the industry is public health."

GRI in Action

The Global Reporting Initiative (GRI) acts in partnership with the UN Global Compact, the OECD, large NGOs active in different areas that overlap with the responsibilities of companies, and others. The guidelines can be used rather like an accounting standard to determine the areas on which to report, and what information should be given. Unlike the 10 principles of the Global Compact, they produce a detailed template for reporting, which is an excellent way to get started in the area of measuring social responsibility performance.

All GRI participation is voluntary, and a participating company sets its own level of compliance. For companies starting out in CSR measurement, GRI recommends a five-step process. First, the overall scope of the engagement is agreed, and an action plan is prepared to manage the process of gathering data and reporting it. The next step is working out what the issues are that matter both to the business internally and to external stakeholders. This involves consultation and discussion, and the issues in question will vary greatly from one company to another. Once all the issues have been identified, the third step is working out a credible way of measuring the company's progress towards implementing best practice. This also involves an internal consultation process to establish specific goals and ways of monitoring performance in each area of the business that has been identified by the stakeholders as important. So, for example, if the issue in question is waste and packaging, the key indicator to be reported could be the amount of packaging used every year, the amount recycled, or the reduction year on year in percentage terms. The next stage is a monitoring process during which the required data is gathered and, finally, the fifth step is the production of the report, which is generally repeated on an annual basis thereafter.

GRI provide detailed reporting guidelines on their website.[54] Firms can choose to account at levels A, B or C, depending on the level of detail they wish to give in each area. For example, firms operating at level C can choose a minimum of 10 performance indicators to measure, spread over economic, social and environmental categories. At level A, companies are required to disclose all such indicators. This level of guidance is very useful, particularly

---

[54] The most recent of these guidelines is available at https://www.globalreporting .org/resourcelibrary/G3.1-Sustainability-Reporting-Guidelines.pdf; last accessed 10 April 2012.

for smaller firms, who are best advised to start off at Level C, and then decide whether or not they wish to move up the chain in the future.[55]

SA8000

SA8000 is a social accounting standard developed and implemented by Social Accountability International (SAI), a large NGO with a particular focus on workers' rights. SA8000 is based on ILO and UN standards, and functions like a quality standard in that it is intended to be independently verified by outside auditors. In the case of SA8000, the independent verification service is offered by SAI's sister organization, Social Accountability Accreditation Services (SAAS), or one of the auditing bodies it has accredited. A company or, more typically, a manufacturing facility, can be accredited for a period of three years, with periodic inspections during that time to maintain their accreditation. The cost of accreditation varies depending on who provides the accreditation, how long it takes, etc. Having the accreditation provides a great deal of reassurance to buyers, however, and it is a useful measure for companies operating in countries that do not offer as much worker protection as their home country. It is common for large US customers to insist that manufacturing plants in countries where there is concern about labour standards have this certification, as this allows them to be more confident about their supply chain. Nevertheless, because SA8000 focuses on labour issues only, it is more limited in scope than other standards.

The International Organisation for Standardisation

A more recent entrant into the field of CSR standards is the International Organisation for Standardisation (ISO),[56] which, as the body behind the familiar ISO quality standards, is a well-respected name in the field of international standards and regulations. Published in late 2010, ISO 26000 covers Social Responsibility, and looks across three main areas of sustainability:

- Economic
- Social
- Environmental

---

[55] Some good examples of GRI reports can be seen at https://www.globalreporting .org/reporting/report-services/featured-reports/Pages/default.aspx; last accessed 10 April 2012.

[56] See www.iso.org; last accessed 10 April 2012.

While ISO 26000 is a good source of guidance on the whole area of CSR, interestingly, it is not produced as a certifiable standard. This means that unlike, for example, the more familiar ISO 9000 standards on quality, a company cannot be certified as complying with or conforming to ISO 26000. It summarises the extant literature on best practice, but does not provide any testable measures which lend themselves to auditing. This was a deliberate choice by ISO; in fact, the organisation has said it will take legal action against anyone claiming to certify the standard for clients, arguing that this is contrary to the spirit of the standard.

As you might expect, ISO 26000 is a carefully drafted document, providing a good introduction to the area of social responsibility and clear definitions. The fact that companies cannot claim it as their own by becoming certified, however, may limit its adoption, or 'traction', worldwide. It is a useful read, but not implementable in the same way as the GRI guidelines.

Other Standards

As well as the global standards for CSR and sustainability outlined above, there is a wide range of industry, geographic or topic-specific standards available to companies. The most useful of these are sincere efforts to address issues of social or environmental concern with a multi-stakeholder approach. A good example is the cocoa industry's response to the issue of forced labour highlighted in the Cadbury case in **Exhibit 3**, or the Kimberly Process, as discussed in **Chapter 3**, which aims to eliminate the flow of conflict diamonds.

In Ireland, a new standard has recently been introduced by Business in the Community Ireland (BITCI), as profiled in **Chapter 3**. This is to be a certifiable standard, audited by the National Standards Authority of Ireland (NSAI), and is currently open only to companies employing at least 250 employees.

Less useful are those standards which are introduced by industry groups, or by bodies heavily influenced by vested interests. For example, there is widespread scepticism in Europe around food labelling, and the process by which labelling regulations are formed. In the UK, Ramesh (2010) describes changes made by the Health Secretary to the Food Safety Authority in a *Guardian* article subtitled "Victory for food manufacturers as health groups accuse Andrew Lansley of caving in to big business." When businesses are too heavily involved in the standard-setting process, there are fears that their motivations may be an effort to water down the impact of future regulation, and make compliance easier.

There are now dozens of potential standards available with which a business can choose to comply, and hundreds of consulting firms who would be happy to offer accreditation services. Firms need to choose carefully who they work with, so as to attain the greatest benefit from the process. If possible, it is most worthwhile to choose those standards with the best global recognition, high traction in terms of being applied widely, and high sanction in terms of facilitating a real benchmarking and improvement process for the business. Some CSR consultants are NGOs or quasi-academic groups; some are privately-held organisations whose main aim is providing networking events for their members; while other CSR-focused organisations operate as whistleblowers, highlighting what they see as bad practice. To a certain extent, because the discipline is so young, there is a scramble to act as gatekeeper to the field; to become the go-to organisation in CSR. This is good, in that it produces a great deal of energy and work in the field. However, not all standards are equally useful. In this, as in so many areas, a slow and thoughtful approach is best.

The good side of the explosion in CSR-focused groups is that there is more and more free information available to interested parties online. For example, www.csrwire.com and www.bsr.org are both good general sources of news on CSR and sustainability. The Ethical Corporation at www.ethicalcorp.com does a similar job, though much of its material is subscription-based. The SEED Initiative at www.seedinit.org highlights good practice in developing countries among start-ups and very small firms, and is a good resource for firms looking for new ideas. There is no shortage of useful information for anyone interested in CSR.

The overall message on CSR measurement is that there is a range of ways in which organisations, even the smallest of businesses, can start to get involved. The UN Global Compact is a good and inexpensive place to start, allowing firms to sign up to key principles, raise awareness internally within an organisation and externally with key stakeholders. The next logical step would be to engage on some level with GRI, either by applying the guidelines as outlines in their free guidance notes, or as a first step by taking what works from their system and applying it to a firm, without the commitment of annual reporting. All steps towards the measurement of a firm's CSR performance are progress in the right direction, so there is nothing wrong with starting small, and working towards more complete disclosure.

Chapter 6

Reporting on CSR

Advantages of External CSR Reporting

There are a number of advantages to providing CSR information outside of a firm. First, it can enhance the reputation of the firm which, in turn, can lead to an increase in turnover, access to socially responsible investment funds (see **Chapter 8**) and the firm being seen as a more desirable place to work, with all the benefits of higher trust and increased social capital locally. Secondly, the consultation process with stakeholders can lead to a closer relationship with key suppliers, customers, regulators, etc. Thirdly, reporting has an internal impact. The very act of reporting on key CSR indicators can change the way in which an entire organisation perceives the issue. It is well known in accounting that what gets measured gets attention; if all the units in a firm need to produce information for a CSR report, as well as for financial statements, this will alter the way in which the issues are regarded and the importance attached to them. This can be seen in action in the Kenmare Resources case profiled in **Part II (Case B)**. Kenmare require community, environmental and safety statistics to be included in every report from their mine in Mozambique, and put this on a par with production information. As Deirdre Corcoran said:

> "It's the first part of any report, so, again, the fact that we require that drives its importance."

Fourthly, since most CSR initiatives lead directly or indirectly to increased profitability or reduced risk, the more attention that a firm pays to indicators on their success year on year, the more carefully they will be implemented, with a knock-on impact on the overall performance of the firm. Finally, limited CSR reporting has already been mandatory for quite some time, particularly in the area of environmental performance. An early example of such legislation is section 299(1)(f) of the Corporations Act, as of 1 July 1998 requiring some Australian companies to disclose details of their performance in relation to environmental regulation. There is a trend towards making more CSR reporting mandatory. For example, in late 2010, California passed the

California Transparency in Supply Chains Act of 2010,[57] which requires all firms with a base in California meeting certain turnover limits to report publicly on the steps they are taking to ascertain whether or not forced labour has been used in their supply chain.

Forms of External CSR Reports

External reporting on CSR takes many forms and, in reporting, many firms use the terms 'CSR' and 'sustainability' interchangeably. Some firms have a simple aspiration towards sustainability or environmental care on their webpage or in their annual report. Others provide incredibly detailed information on how the business is doing in working towards predefined goals. To a large extent, the more detail that is provided, the more credible the overall message is. After all, if an organisation is serious about improving CSR performance, it will be monitoring the issue internally. If that is the case, why not avail of the reputational benefit by also reporting to outside stakeholders? If an organisation has consulted stakeholders and chosen standards with which it can comply, and taken steps to measure performance on key indicators, the next logical step is compiling a report and communicating it externally.

Exhibit 13: Signalling Theory Applied

A CSR report produced for people outside a firm is intended to convey real information about what is going on inside the company to people who are relatively uninformed. One way of ensuring the report does so in a way that is believable is to make it conform to the principles of signalling theory, a theory developed by US economist Michael Spence.

His study (Spence, 1973) looked at the job market for graduates. He described how all graduates applying for a job looked similar to potential employers, presenting with the same basic qualification – their college degree. However, some of them were better candidates than others, in ways that were not always obvious from their qualifications. The graduates themselves knew if they were good or bad candidates for the job, but the potential employers did not. This scenario, where

---

[57] See http://info.sen.ca.gov/pub/09-10/bill/sen/sb_0651-0700/sb_657_bill_20100930_
chaptered.html; last accessed 15 May 2012.

one party to a transaction has more key information than the other, is often referred to as 'information asymmetry'. Spence studied the most effective ways to overcome such information asymmetry and isolated four characteristics of what he called effective 'signalling'. A 'signal', as Spence understood it, was a way for the better graduates to convey information about their skills to potential employers in a way that is credible, and distinguishes them from others. Spence found that a good signal should have four characteristics. It should be:

- credible;
- verifiable;
- easy to understand; and
- hard for weaker candidates/competitors to copy.

In the context of a job applicant, an effective signal of strong leadership skills might be the fact that the student had captained a sports team or led a major project while in college. A part-time job could be a good signal of a work ethic or of people skills, depending on the nature of the work.

It is possible to apply these four criteria to CSR reports, to see what characteristics they should have if they are to serve as effective signals of the good work undertaken by a firm. A simple statement that the firm is committed to the principles of the UN Global Compact is not verifiable or difficult for weaker firms to copy. As such, it is not a convincing signal. On the other hand, detailed reporting with year-on-year progress on key indicators following, for example, the GRI structure is an excellent signal, particularly if externally audited. It follows that this form of reporting will have more credibility, and so is more likely to have a positive impact on the reputation of a firm.

The process of preparing a report along the lines of the Global Reporting Initiative is described above in **Chapter 5.** However, in all external reporting there is a real opportunity to move beyond the dry facts and figures and project a sense of what your organisation is really all about. Some companies have a very strong public persona. Innocent Drinks, who make Innocent juices and smoothies, promotes an image of simplicity, a passion for pure food and care for the environment. This is conveyed not only in the text of their sustainability report[58] but also in the choice of an informal font, the use

---

[58] Available online at http://assets.innocentdrinks.co.uk/innocentsustainability.pdf; last accessed 16 April 2012.

of simple graphics like the drawings of a child, and the expression of the report in informal language. For example, in describing the need for site visits to suppliers the report says:

> "Sure you can get to know someone over the internet, or even on the phone, but we all know that eventually you have to meet face to face before you really get to know them. It's exactly the same for us with our farmers – there is just no substitute for a face to face chat to make sure that we properly understand what it's like to grow strawberries in Poland for example and the kind of challenges they face to produce a great crop, look after their workers and protect the environment."

Ben & Jerry's Ice Cream is a company that actively promotes a wide range of social causes from gay marriage to support for the Occupy Wall Street movement. They retain their distinctive personality despite being taken over by Unilever in April 2000. Their Social and Environmental Assessment Reports[59] include a wide range of metrics updated annually on issues such as the ingredients used in their ice cream products, the use of minority suppliers, their liveable wage policy, community involvement and activism, etc. Both Ben & Jerry's Ice Cream and Innocent Drinks are good examples of how a CSR report can be used to convey more than the raw data on an organisation's performance on CSR metrics.

For SMEs, involving as many employees as possible can be a way of reflecting the informality that generally permeates smaller firms to convey a sense of the company as a community of people. An excellent example is the clothing company Impahla, South Africa's "first carbon neutral garment manufacturer". While they do not produce a CSR or sustainability report on an annual basis, their most recent offering, the *Sustainability Report 2009*,[60] is full of photos of employees, as well as a candid report card highlighting the targets they reached and those they failed to attain, with detailed explanations. For example, on page 2 of the report the following information is given:

✓ Became the first carbon neutral garment manufacturer in South Africa through an effective carbon offset partnership with Food & Trees for Africa, and with the help of Carbon Calculated

---

59   Available online at http://www.benjerry.com/company/sear/2010/index.cfm; last accessed 16 April 2012.

60   The Impahla Clothing *Sustainability Report 2009* is available online at http://safe .puma.com/us/en/wp-content/uploads/imphala_2009.pdf; last accessed 16 April 2012.

✗ Experienced a marked increase in the number of non-lost time injuries (NLTI) – 28 – during 2009, up from 16 in 2008, and only one in 2007

✗ Although committed to the procurement of local (i.e. South African) goods and services, unless unavailable in sufficient quality or quantity, 58.9% of all fabric purchased in 2009 was foreign

✓ 100% of all cotton is procured from South African suppliers and has at least 5% organic content

✓ Recorded an absenteeism rate of 2.40% for the year, well below local and national trade benchmarks of 6.0%, and a 10.4% improvement over our 2008 absenteeism rate of 2.68%

Their honesty is disarming. As a report, it does far more than simply cata-logue the score of the company with regard to CSR metrics. It acts as a pow-erful marketing tool, giving the reader the sense of a company trying to achieve a great deal, and succeeding in some of it. The inclusion of goals they have not reached makes the whole report seem more sincere, and makes the company appear likeable in some way.

Ideally, a sustainability or CSR report should be integrated into the other annual reports produced by the organisation. If the company formally pro-duces an annual financial report, it could follow the lead of Danish Pharma-ceutical company, Novo Nordisk, and integrate the sustainability information, giving it equal weight.[61] Some US companies that report financial information quarterly also produce a quarterly sustainability report. For example, the out-door clothing company Timberland produce a *Timberland Responsibility* report,[62] updating a wide range of indicators on a quarterly basis.

Obviously, this is quite labour-intensive, and beyond the reach of most SMEs. However, there are many simpler options for timely reporting. Social media can easily be used to convey informal CSR and sustainability informa-tion on an ongoing basis. Twitter and Facebook have wide reach, and can operate more or less in real time. A good Facebook presence, updated in a friendly manner every couple of days is a useful tool. Twitter is an excellent way of broadcasting short bursts of information, making links with like-minded firms or stakeholders, and receiving instant feedback. Despite their inherent informality, it is important to be consistent, and to ensure that the voice of the company that comes through on social media is responsible and thoughtful. It's also important to include useful contact information in the company profile and, above all, to listen as well as speak.

---

[61] See the NovoNordisk 2010 annual report online at http://annualreport2010 .novonordisk.com; last accessed 16 April 2012.

[62] Available online at http://responsibility.timberland.com/reporting/goals-and-progress/; last accessed 16 April 2012.

Some very successful CSR and sustainability reporting does not publicise the key indicators used to measure progress and performance, and some reports do not include key performance indicators at all. For example, the Innocent Drinks report referenced above explains that the company has developed its own standards based, *inter alia*, on SA8000 and Fairtrade. However, while they report progress towards some goals, the goals themselves are not quantified. Obviously, applying Spence's signalling theory, this weakens the credibility of the message. A good example of a largely non-quantitative but very well-regarded report[63] is that of Westpac, a large Australian bank with an excellent reputation for sustainability. They highlight, for example, awards given during the year in the social and environmental fields, rather than detailed measures of their own internal performance. By reporting an external validation, they achieve more credibility in their message.

CSR, social, and environmental and sustainability reports have been presented in a whimsical way, such as the multimedia website used by Manchester City Football Club. Designed to be like an online game, the 'reader' interacts with a plan of the city, discovering the impact of the Club on many aspects of community life.[64] Some CSR reports can be very short, while others are long and detailed and comply rigorously with the GRI guidelines.

The best reports, however, present at least some of the struggles that a company has in reaching its CSR targets, and admit to imperfections where they exist. Apart from being more credible, as in the case of Impahla Clothing highlighted above, it is a safer and more conservative strategy to err on the side of understatement in social achievements. An interesting European example of a company which openly discusses its internal struggles is Rabobank, which sets out a series of ethical dilemmas faced by the group over the year, and the issues they weighed in deciding what action to take.[65] Few financial institutions would instinctively make this kind of information available publicly. Doing so enhances Rabobank's reputation as being open and straightforward, giving it a clear competitive advantage at a time

---

[63] See their report online at http://www.westpac.com.au/about-westpac/sustainability-and-community/; last accessed 16 April 2012.

[64] The interactive report is available at http://csr.mcfc.co.uk; last accessed 16 April 2012.

[65] See http://www.rabobank.com/content/csr/ethics_and_issues/; last accessed 16 April 2012.

when trust in banks generally is low. Interestingly, such an approach is only really possible when the management have a conscious strategy for dealing with these business dilemmas. Publishing the dilemmas then is a strategy that is difficult for competitors to copy, and so conforms with the most important of Spence's signalling criteria. This is partly what makes it so convincing.

Once a report of this kind has been prepared, the next step is to publicise it, and make it available to as wide a range of stakeholders as possible. Here, there are as many options as you can imagine, from the traditional printed report to a lively Twitter account. Ironically, however, many companies put far more effort into drawing up their CSR or sustainability report than into communicating it.

Conclusion

Once a company begins to report, it is important to continue on a regular basis – at least every two years. Otherwise, the impression can be given that CSR or sustainability is only something that the firm cared about in the past. For this reason alone, it is best to start relatively small, and ensure that the workload in producing a report is set at a level that can be repeated in the following year. It is also important to choose at least some real measures that are internal to the company but can be disclosed without compromising business confidentiality. This gives more credibility to the report, and makes it something personal to the firm. The overall style of the report should be carefully chosen to reflect the image of the company, but it should be similar enough in tone to the company's annual report to show that CSR is taken seriously.

Finally, it is important not to give hostages to fortune by making inflated or grand claims, which could be challenged in the court of public opinion. Once the report is released, it will be read widely, so a firm should report only on what it can honestly stand over in public discussion.

Chapter 7

CSR in Smaller Enterprises

As we have seen, CSR is often seen as something that mainly applies to large, multinational firms. These are the organisations most likely to have a clearly-articulated CSR strategy and a section on their website devoted to explaining how it is being implemented. Certainly, they are more likely to report on an annual basis, or to 'fly the flag' as David O'Mahony of O'Mahony Books puts it (see **Case C** in **Part II**). However, as has been outlined earlier, this does not mean that multinationals carry more responsibilities than smaller firms.

The Importance of Responsibility in SMEs

SMEs have an enormous collective impact. Taking Ireland as an example, it is true that large firms account for most of the GDP, as noted, *inter alia*, by the EC (2008) report based on 2005 figures from the Eurostat SBS data base. However, the same report observes that over 99% of businesses in Ireland were SMEs or microenterprises, and that these accounted for two-thirds of all people employed in the private sector.[66] These figures are echoed in the Tax Strategy (2006) report, which excludes public sector and agriculture from its considerations and finds that roughly half of all the remaining employees in the country work for firms employing 50 people or less.[67] Most of the very large companies in Ireland are exporters rather than retailers. So, in terms of where people work, where they shop and find their entertainment, and in raw numbers of actual businesses, smaller firms dominate the life of Ireland. As smaller firms collectively act in a more responsible way, this will have a very significant impact on society.

It is important to note that, even though most SMEs do not formally report their CSR activities, or may not even have formalised a CSR focus, they make a massive contribution socially, often without realising it. Smaller businesses are, by their nature, embedded in rather than separate from the

---

[66] See EC (2008).

[67] See Tax Strategy (2006).

community. The examples in **Part II** demonstrate how a wide range of responsible initiatives occur within smaller firms, often in an ad hoc and non-strategic way. For many firms, CSR has simply not been on their radar, and they have not yet begun to think of what they do in terms of CSR. David O'Mahony of O'Mahony's Books (see **Case C** in **Part II**) sums up the position of many smaller firms when he says:

> "It's only when you really think about it and put all the things together that you realise that there's a lot more going on than we would have probably realised ourselves. Things we do in the CSR area are happening in an ad hoc way rather than in a concerted, policy-driven way."

Despite not describing any part of their activities or practices as CSR, smaller firms that are closely knitted into the local business community and wider society may rely more heavily than large firms on trust and reputation. Perhaps, for this reason, studies such as that undertaken by Mandl and Dorr (2005) report a comparatively high level of ethics and moral accountability among the owners of smaller firms.

Why Smaller Firms do not Report CSR

Despite their evident moral accountability, it is clear that many SMEs do not think about CSR to the same extent as larger firms and, certainly, are far less likely to report their CSR or sustainability information outside of the firm. Of the eight businesses profiled in **Part II**, only Kenmare Resources (see **Case B**) – the largest of the firms and the only one listed on a stock exchange – reports its CSR activities externally. None of the seven smaller firms does so in a formal way. The main reason why smaller firms are less likely to report their CSR activities very often comes down to not feeling the need to do so. A publicly-quoted firm, on the other hand, has a constant eye to the financial markets and is always keen to promote its image to a wide range of stakeholders.

SMEs tend to have far less separation of ownership and control. This has profound implications for the information flows within an organisation. With an owner–manager, the need for internal and external reporting is reduced, because the main shareholder already understands very well what is going on in the business. Unless the organisation is considering raising external finance in the near future, there is little need to consider how potential investors might perceive the company. The focus in private firms, as shown by the following quotes from SMEs profiled in **Part II**, is on the customer. If there is a perception that the customer is not interested in the CSR activities of the company, these will not be reported:

> "I don't think it's a huge selling point. Price and style are what people are looking for here. If they can salve their conscience at the same time, then that's all well and good, but I don't think it's a purchasing decision for an awful lot of people." – **Gerry Brannigan of Blackfield Clothing** (see **Case D** in **Part II**).

> "That ethos is really important, but I don't put it on our website because I don't think it's really of value relevance to people. That's just how we run the business internally." – **Brendan Salmon of KPS Colourprint** (see **Case A** in **Part II**).

Other smaller firms have a strategy around CSR, but have not yet found a credible way of reporting it. For example, Nova Partners (see **Case E** in **Part II**) have a strategy to differentiate themselves in terms of the transparency of their pricing, but do not yet couch this in terms of CSR:

> "We don't really report that ethos of transparency on our website. We do say we're customer-focused, but so does everyone. I think the proof is in the pudding and, as our clients experience what we offer, that will get the message out. We don't look to CSR standards really, though that could be an interesting thing to do in the future." – **Noreen Clifford of Nova Partners**.

At the moment, Nova Partners are relying on word-of-mouth to build their reputation, though they recognise that formally reporting what they do, and complying with external standards would be more effective.

Often, however, the decision not to report comes down to time and resources. Tollymore Outdoor Centre (see **Case F** in **Part II**) already report in a limited way, but plan to do more, constrained by resources:

> "We have reported our CSR on the website, but I guess we don't sell it enough ... A critical resource that we are missing just now is people to get us to our target levels ... That is certainly an area we can do a lot more in." – **Turlough O'Gorman of Tollymore Outdoor Centre**.

Smaller companies are also far less aware of CSR standards, perhaps because their peers are not yet using them to report:

> "We focus on doing the right thing, and the motivation for that comes from within, not from outside. I didn't even know there were CSR standards out there." – **Colm O'Brien of Carambola** (see **Case H** in **Part II**).

Since many of the standards, as discussed in the previous chapter, lend themselves to the preparation of an external report, a lack of familiarity with the standards means that the idea of external reporting is less likely to be on the radar of business leaders.

Small firms are closer to the community, as they may function in locally-based business environments and be part of local networks with other non-competing firms. In doing so, they are engaging in a wide range of outreach activities. For example, they are likely to be involved in industry groups and, on a personal level, the senior managers may be active in community organisations. For example, Mary Fitzgerald of the Woodland House Hotel (see **Case G** in **Part II**) says:

> "On a personal level, I am involved with dozens of organisations locally. That's my bit for the community, for society. My staff can see me getting involved personally like that, so it sets the pace."

Her involvement in local community-based organisations is not seen by her as something separate from the responsible orientation of the hotel; nor would it be described by her as a CSR activity.

The owners and directors of many smaller businesses behave in a community-oriented way because this seems natural, to them, perhaps based on the values of their family of origin. This came up again and again in the businesses profiled in **Part II**:

> "A lot of what we do, we do this way because of the way we were brought up."[68]

The profiled business owners almost never referred to formal codes of ethics, instead citing personal values such as, "We are all human beings;"[69] "These things are personal";[70] or by referring to some irresponsible behaviour as "a clash with our own values".[71] Perhaps because the leaders in smaller firms have the opportunity to match the ethos of the firm with their own, they do not need to think in terms of a separate set of values for the business. In turn, this focus on the internal values of the leader arguably makes the values that define the firm less likely to be written down and reported.

Because of their size, SMEs tend to be less formal in their internal relations. They may have less-specialised staff, preferring to be able to deploy

---

[68] David O'Mahony of O'Mahony's Books – **Part II, Case C.**
[69] Brendan Salmon of KPS Colourprint – **Part II, Case A.**
[70] Gerry Brannigan of Blackfield – **Part II, Case D.**
[71] Noreen Clifford of Nova Partners – **Part II, Case E.**

people to the area of most need at a given time. This means less documentation around role descriptions and less articulation of the way in which business should be conducted. For example, in a small retail outlet, a new cashier is likely to be personally trained by the owner and told how to respond to customers, handle cash or deal with risks. The procedures can be excellent, but remain largely unarticulated, and certainly undocumented. In a large retail chain, these procedures would be written down. With less documentation overall in small firms, there is less on hand with which to put together a CSR report.

EXHIBIT 14: EUROPEAN EXAMPLES OF SME ENGAGEMENT WITH CSR

The EU has collected some interesting examples of SME engagement with CSR, highlighting particular initiatives from different countries. Mandl and Dorr (2005) summarise their findings. Here are just three examples:

The German medium-sized cleaning company, LR Gebäudereinigung, among others, provides cost-free German classes for its employees who have come to Germany from other countries. It also organises workshops on environmental issues on an annual basis for its trainees. This has a number of advantages for all parties. The employees improve their language skills, and get to know each other better, which reduces alienation for people moving to a new place. For the employer, it creates a better team spirit and a more skilled workforce. Furthermore, they have used some of the ideas that have come from the environmental workshops as part of the company's environmental strategy.

Protu AS, a micro IT enterprise in Norway, provides mobile phones and broadband home Internet connections to all its employees, free of charge, ensuring that all employees have a fully-serviced home office. The follow-through is that the company does not keep a record of how many days an employee might spend at home due to illness or their children's illness, focusing instead on the individual's output rather than days attended on the premises. The employees can thus take as much time as they wish to recover, but are in a position to work while caring for sick children at home. The company was motivated by the burnout associated with IT workers in their competitors. The rationale is that if the employees perceive their work as fun, and have a well-adjusted work-life balance, they will be more willing workers, more loyal, and more productive overall.

The Romanian research company, SC Icemenerg SA, assigns 5% of its turnover to measures aimed at improving the employees' working conditions. Recent examples of how this has been spent include investing in social events, training in occupational health, and work on the provision of an employee recreation centre. The company reports that both morale and the public image of the company have improved.[72]

Why SMEs Should Report

Over time, most SMEs will come to see the value of external reporting of one form or another. As Colm O'Brien of Carambola (see Case **H** in **Part II**) put it, "It's good business to do the right thing." It is likely that this will be driven, to a large extent, by outside stakeholders, particularly customers or, as noted by Mandl and Dorr (2005), business partners or peers.

There is a competitive advantage to be gained from reporting. In a recession, a small firm's main advantage is its personal touch. This "personality" needs to be reported externally if it is to reach the potential customers who are actively shopping online. The previous chapter has shown how CSR and sustainability reporting can effectively convey a sense of what the company is all about.

A CSR and sustainability report, even one that is relatively slight initially, can be effectively used to renew the image of a company, particularly around the launch of new products or services. All in all, CSR and sustainability is probably reasonably well-embedded within smaller firms, with their increased reliance on trust and personal integrity. Reporting on this can convey this ethos effectively to customers and other potential partners. Reporting can also greatly facilitate promotion of the values within a firm, although this is less of a concern in small firms.

---

[72] Source: "CSR and Competitiveness – European SMEs' Good Practice" EU-funded research project led by Austrian Institute for SME Research (KMU FORSCHUNG AUSTRIA).

Finally, SMEs need to consider formalising their CSR information because there is an increasing trend for external reporting among their peers. The level of engagement of SMEs in CSR still varies in different countries. For example, Mandl and Dorr (2005: 7) report that "83% of Finnish SMEs are engaged in CSR whereas 'only' 46% of Spanish SMEs conduct such activities." The trend overall is upwards. Sooner or later most sectors will see a great deal more CSR and sustainability reporting. Firms which start now can only gain first-mover advantage in the area.

Responsibilities of Smaller Firms

While the same basic responsibilities apply to all firms, there are some key differences[73] between SMEs and large multinational firms, which impact on the practical application of CSR policy for an SME.

The differences that are relevant to the responsibilities of the firm are not so much size and number of employees, but centre on the relative power of individual SMEs *vis-à-vis* larger multinational firms. The easiest way to understand this is to look at a specific responsibility. Take the supply chain, for example. Large multinationals, such as GAP and Nike in the US, have been held responsible for the basic employee rights and human rights of workers at externally-owned factories in which their goods are produced. (See also the case of Apple referred to in **Chapter 4**.)

In the case of Nike, as described in Stabile (2000), the widespread boycott in the 1980s had the effect of raising consumer awareness and indirectly improving conditions across the whole sports shoe industry. GAP's response to reports that their clothes were produced in sweatshop conditions was to put in place an internal team of monitors who visit all factories regularly, and impose a vendor code of conduct.

Nevertheless, sweatshops continue to produce consumer goods for a wide range of suppliers. A recent report by the International Textile Garment and Leather Workers' Federation (ITGLWF, 2011) looked at the production of sportswear in three countries – Sri Lanka, Indonesia and The Philippines – surveying factories employing a total of 100,000 workers. They found shocking conditions, where none of the respondents paid a living wage, most workers were on short-term contracts, and overtime was excessive and forced. For many SMEs, this means that, unless they take steps to assure

---

[73] For a good discussion on CSR for smaller firms, see Jenkins (2006).

themselves of the origin of the goods they sell, it is likely that they are produced in sweatshop conditions.

However, is it fair that a small business in Ireland, for example, should be held as responsible for the conditions in businesses up the supply chain as a global multinational such as GAP? Smaller firms do not have the resources of a company like GAP, and cannot put in place an internal group to monitor conditions in their suppliers' factories. Neither do they have the buying power to impose a code of conduct on their suppliers. What then are their responsibilities for the conditions under which the goods they sell are produced?

As previously noted, the ILO have stated that a firm has responsibility as far up the supply chain as it has "reasonable influence". This means that if you are the company's largest customer, or a massive player in the market, it is reasonable to assume that you have significant influence over your suppliers. Best practice then dictates that you should use that influence as far as you can to ensure that these suppliers are behaving responsibly in terms of the way in which they produce the goods you sell. A good example here is Starbucks, who actively work with their coffee producers to bring them up to Fairtrade standards. If, on the other hand, you are a very small trader, buying only small amounts of goods, you do not have the same influence and, so, your responsibility is limited to the choices you make, and the use of your influence as far as it is practical.

A fitting example of good practice on supply chain issues is the purchasing policy of Blackfield Clothing and Surf School, featured in **Part II**. As Gerry Brannigan puts it:

> "We also know that there are certain products that we get from certain companies, and goodness knows where they come from … If somebody came to us and said, 'Look, we know for sure that this is being made in a sweatshop in India,' then we would say, 'We can't touch that.' We have worked with Fairtrade companies sourcing jewellery especially…"

Blackfield actively seeks to do the right thing in terms of purchasing where they can, and to make choices to reflect the values they hold, but accepts that there are areas over which they are simply too small to have any influence. In this sense, Blackfield's policy on sourcing its goods as described above, while very loosely articulated, is a fine example of responsible supply chain management from a small business.

The key difference between the scope of responsibility for the supply chain in a large or a small firm hinges then on a firm's level of power and control. This also applies in other areas of CSR. Extending the idea that with influence comes responsibility, it follows that smaller firms have the same responsibilities of larger ones in areas they can control, such as fair pricing, labour issues, the promotion and protection of human rights within their own organisation and, as far as possible, outside of it, and so on. The key question to ask in each field of CSR is this: "Is the company doing all that it reasonably can to achieve best practice in this area?" If the answer is yes, then a smaller firm can be said to be fulfilling its responsibilities, even if the result is less than perfection.

Conclusion

In summary, while CSR is often seen as the domain of larger multinational firms, SMEs, because of their impact on society, are potentially more important players in the area. Many smaller firms do not formalise their CSR policies for a number of reasons, including informality, pressure of time and resources, unfamiliarity with external standards and a strong internal locus of ethics vested in the leaders. In fact, however, smaller firms that operate on trust and informality are likely to have high levels of engagement with their local communities and to operate in a responsible manner on an intuitive basis, drawing on personal values. This is the essence of virtue-based ethics – that sense of "who we are" rather than "what we have decided to do". It is important that SMEs move towards recording and reporting this, so as to gain competitive advantage, and to ingrain this ethos in the firm outside of the personal values of the owner/managers. While there are areas in which smaller firms have less power and, so, fewer direct responsibilities than large companies, the key to social responsibility lies in doing whatever is within your power to achieve best practice in each area of CSR.

Chapter 8

The Future of CSR

The evolution of CSR will be driven in the future by key trends that are already underway. The global supply of goods and services, improvements in broadband access and reduced regulation on the sale of goods has led to a sharp increase in online shopping, and to better-informed consumers. This in turn increases competition among all firms. Consumers are increasingly willing to shop around, buy online, or at least to use the Internet to establish a price against which to benchmark goods and services. This represents a move away from the older, relationship-based selling, where a particular merchant was the source of particular goods, and price was either not competitive or not a key determinant in purchasing choices. If a business is to distinguish itself and gain competitive advantage in this new, fast-moving world, it is important to establish a strong identity, and pay attention to the image of the firm. This factor alone will drive more CSR activity in business.

All other things being equal, people will buy from someone they trust, though trust is itself a contested concept – see **Exhibit 15** below. Even if things are not quite so equal, customers in both the business and private sector may be willing to pay a certain premium to deal with a firm they feel will deal with them honestly. So, it is important to be considered trustworthy. In general, smaller, local firms are more trusted than international brands, simply because the owners of these firms may be personally known to customers. The trust is based on interpersonal relationships rather than a corporate identity. Few SMEs actually leverage this, however, by articulating their sense of identity within the community on their websites or their corporate literature. With increasing competition, it is likely that more attention will be paid by smaller firms to brand image, and so CSR and sustainability reporting will become a trend.

EXHIBIT 15: TRUST

The question of trust – what it means and how to measure it – is contested, yet indices measuring the relative amount of trust placed by the public in particular organisations, professions, leaders or brands are widely reported, and are broadly taken at face value. The best known is the Edelman Trust Barometer,[74] which comes out annually. The Trust Barometer is based on a survey of more than 30,000 people worldwide. The results are useful not so much in absolute terms – what does it mean, after all, to say that 67% of employees rank a technical expert within a company as more credible than a CEO? – but rather in mapping trends from year to year. So, for example, the 2012 results show the most marked drop ever in trust in CEOs. This information can be useful to social commentators, and to organisations interested in how to convey a particular message in a way that is credible.

Despite the widespread acceptance of the Edelman Trust Barometer, however, the methodology of trust surveys can be questionable. Most trust measures are based on fairly straightforward survey questions, asking the respondents to rate the amount of trust they place in a range of occupations or categories. They generally ask a fairly simple question such as: "How much do you trust businesses to do what is right?" The difficulty with this is that trust really depends on the context. If we are presented with an image of a grimy back-alley, frequented by small-time criminals, and we are asked the question: "How likely would you be to trust someone you had never met before with your possessions?" we would probably answer at the low end of the scale. However, in the context of an up-market hotel, where a concierge waits to take our jacket and our keys, we might answer differently. We trust strangers if they are wearing white coats and standing over our hospital beds more than we do if they are poorly dressed and loitering near our cars. So, a survey that is filled in by the respondent in an unknown context is a limited methodology.

Secondly, "trust" is a word that simply covers too much to be used alone. If a survey asks, "Do you trust large corporations?" it does not allow for any level of detail on why you might trust them, in what circumstances, or with what. This difficulty is most easily illustrated by the old joke, "I trust my dog with my life, but not with my ham sandwich." If someone answers that they trust a corporation or a brand to

---

[74] The results are available online at: www.edelman.com/trust; last accessed 18 April 2012.

do the right thing, which question are they answering? Do I trust a particular company to make safe products? To stay in business? To act in accordance with its brand image? To safeguard the economy? To employ more workers or pay higher dividends?

Nevertheless, trust surveys, particularly those that are repeated year on year with the same methodology, present a snapshot of trends in trust.

A second important trend going forward will be an increase in the implementation by businesses of impact assessments in the area of CSR. An impact assessment is an effort to measure the entire impact of a particular initiative, project or even an entire business on a local area, a supply chain or the environment. Impact assessments can be done in specific areas such as human rights[75] or the environment, but, increasingly, a holistic assessment for the firm will become a feature of CSR reporting. By virtue of their scale and scope, impact assessments can be complex and difficult. In general, they are done by an outside accrediting body, and there are a number of consulting firms and some NGOs who undertake this work for a fee. Impact assessments are still very much niche products. However, as the methodology improves, and they become easier and less expensive to carry out, they are likely to become more mainstream as a way for the best firms to differentiate themselves from their competitors.

It is also likely that we will see more and more meaningful stakeholder engagement. This is part of a trend that is already on-going. For example, it is more common now than it was 20 years ago for a firm to run customer focus groups, employee satisfaction surveys, etc. As firms listen more to their stakeholders, they will be better able to identify the issues of importance to them and refine their CSR policy accordingly. Firms can also use this engagement to promote their business within the stakeholder group, and improve their reputation generally.

New media and social media will, of course, be important in CSR, as in all forms of communication for business. Social media is particularly important, however, in conveying what has been described as the softer aspects of a company's activities – the social initiatives and outreach work – rather than the

---

[75] See www.humanrightsimpact.org for a collection of useful resources on Human Rights Impact Assessments, many of which can be applied to other areas of a firm's CSR engagement.

hard financial data of performance. As such, it lends itself well to conveying information on CSR activities.

Partnering strategically with relevant NGOs and community groups is already a growing trend for large businesses, and this is expected to continue into the future. Partnering is also a useful strategy for smaller firms if they have an initiative they want to advance locally. Done carefully, with mutual respect between the firm and the NGO, it can be a win-win strategy. (Examples of successful partnering can be seen in the case of Kenmare Resources (**Case B** in **Part II**.)

At present, there is still a plethora of possible reporting standards available to business. Most of these are loosely based in one way or another on the UN Global Compact outlined earlier, and/or the Global Reporting Initiative. As more and more firms begin to report, it is likely that these standards will converge to some extent, making it simpler for companies to report in a standardised way. With this will come more comparable reports, making it easier to assess a firm's real CSR performance. Hopefully, such standardisation will not come at the cost of the honest individuality now present in some SMEs' reports.

EXHIBIT 16: CSR AS EVOLUTION

While most firms start off regarding CSR as essentially about philanthropy or targeted donations to charity, it quickly becomes clear to anyone looking at best practice that it is far more fundamental than that. In recent years, a sort of evolution in the way a business regards CSR has been analysed by academics and commentators as a development process. A good example of this kind of analysis comes from Boston College, where Philip Mirvis, an organizational psychologist, worked with Bradley Googins from the Center for Corporate Citizenship, to map out the stages of development of a company's thinking about CSR (Mirvis and Googins, 2006).

They identify five stages of a company's attitude to CSR, which they label: Elementary, Engaged, Innovative, Integrated and Transforming. A company at the Elementary stage sees citizenship solely in terms of jobs, profit and taxes, is defensive on key issues and disclosure, and focused on legal compliance. At stage two, an Engaged firm will undertake some philanthropy, be reactive to issues that are brought to its attention by consumers or lobbyists, and will see disclosure of CSR primarily as a form of public relations. An Innovative firm at stage three will understand the business case for CSR initiatives, favouring those that have an immediate impact on profit. Such a firm will engage in stakeholder management and public reporting of their CSR initiatives. A firm at stage four has an Integrated approach, and will work in partnership with stakeholders, champion CSR and try to integrate all aspects of the organisation to serve the same goals. A Transforming company at stage five is one that changes the game in their industry. The company's intent at this level is social change of some kind, perhaps within the industry, a target market or the wider community, or the creation of an entirely new market for a different sort of product. A good example of a transforming company is the case of Interface Carpets, profiled below at **Exhibit 17.** The company favours full disclosure of CSR initiatives and challenges, defines new issues rather than simply adopting those that have been brought to it by consumers and NGOs, and works with multiple stakeholders, including regulators, to change the landscape of the industry.

A company may begin its CSR journey at an elementary level by being defensive on contentious issues, defining its main contribution to society in terms of employment, economic activity and taxation, and perhaps engaging in some strategic philanthropic activity at a local level. After spending some time at this level, they may see the public relations value of more strategic disclosure of the CSR activities that they are undertaking. Over time, they may decide to take more action on the CSR initiatives that result in more profit, and begin actively engaging with stakeholders, etc., moving up along the chain towards becoming a transforming firm. Not all organisations will become transforming, of course, but it is really useful to understand the stage a particular company is at, because, as Mirvis and Googins put it:

> "Knowing at what stage a company is, and what challenges it faces in advancing citizenship, can clear up an executive's confusion about where things stand, frame strategic choices about where to go, aid in setting benchmarks and goals, and perhaps speed movement forward."[76]

---

[76] Mirvis and Googins (2006: 3).

As seen in the example of Interface Carpets (**Exhibit 17** below), it is only when CSR and sustainability become part of the strategy of a company, affecting all aspects of its day-to-day operations, that it really begins to make a difference.

As CSR continues to develop, it is likely that new areas will come to the forefront of CSR reporting. For many US firms, the focus has so far been all about the environment because, as noted earlier, environmental initiatives generally save on energy, transport or packaging costs and, so, have an immediate impact on profit. Relatively little attention has been paid to issues of corruption and relations with governments. Since these issues are of increasing importance to the public now – in the current recession – we can expect them to emerge as key differentiators in CSR reporting in the near future. Similarly, energy consumption, water conservation and water rights, and the development or use of renewables will become increasingly significant.

Exhibit 17: Changing Culture at Interface Carpets

Until 1994, it was business as usual at Interface Carpets, a successful American multinational company dealing in modular carpets for commercial customers. The carpet industry generally at that time involved a great deal of waste and very little in the way of recycled materials. Customers began to ask questions about what the company was doing for the environment, and the answer, in the words of Chairman Ray Anderson, was "Not very much."[77] This bothered some people in the organisation, and they formed a taskforce to look into these issues. They asked Ray Anderson to launch the taskforce with a speech setting out his environmental vision. As he later put it: "I didn't have an environmental vision. I did not want to make that speech. And at that propitious moment, this book landed on my desk."

The book was Paul Hawken's *The Ecology of Commerce*.[78] Ray Anderson began to read it to find some inspiration for his speech but, to his

---

[77] All quotes in this section are from Anderson's interview in *The Corporation*, a 2004 film by Achbar, Abbot and Bakan.

[78] Hawken (1994).

surprise, found that it changed the way he looked at the entire business cycle of Interface Carpets. Within a decade, operations at all of the company's manufacturing plants worldwide had been transformed, with the company working towards sustainable production by seeking to mimic the closed loop of nature, where all waste is absorbed back into the ecosystem. The company's aim is now very ambitious: zero waste, all energy used to come from renewable sources, and as much as possible of the waste material to be recycled directly back into the production process.

The implementation of this environmentally focused initiative/strategy has not only changed the company's impact on the environment and given them a distinct edge in an industry not known for having environmental credentials, it has also saved a great deal of cost, and opened up new business opportunities. For example, the company now also leases carpets to large commercial customers, maintaining them and replacing them in a business model similar to that used for fleet cars. This allows the company's customers to enjoy a high quality product, which they are sure is completely sustainable. For Interface, it changes the nature of the supply from goods to a service, which essentially allows them to diversify their business model.

The makeover has not been easy, but it has paid dividends. It has been a complete transformation, affecting all aspects of the business, perhaps because the strategy was born of the genuine conviction of the CEO, and so had support throughout the organisation. As Ray Anderson put it, "Unless we can make carpets sustainably, perhaps we don't have a place in a sustainable world. But neither does anybody else making products unsustainably."

Today, Interface operates in the US, Europe and the Asia-Pacific regions, with approximately 3,500 employees worldwide. The company has 11 manufacturing plants, including four in Europe, and their net sales in 2011 came to just over a US$1 billion.[79]

The role of capital markets may also become more significant in driving the adoption of CSR and reporting of CSR and sustainability in the coming years. Already, there is a significant body of investors and investment funds worldwide concerned with ethical investment. As these Socially Responsible

---

[79] See www.interfaceglobal.com.

Investment funds (SRI funds) become more significant in the market, they can be a useful source of finance for any firm with a well-organised CSR strategy. Their presence is likely, therefore, to incentivise more companies to take on CSR and report it. Furthermore, the development in several major stock exchanges of a separate index based on sustainability or ethical practice is also driving sustainability reporting. A good early example of this is the Johannesburg Stock Exchange's Socially Responsible Investment (SRI) Index,[80] which was launched in 2004. The aim of the Index was to provide a means for investors to identify companies with good practices socially and environmentally, as well as financially, and to provide guidance to companies seeking to improve their performance on all three grounds. The Exchange developed criteria to measure this triple bottom line performance, and compiled an index of companies reaching a threshold standard from those listed on the main exchange. The initiative encourages companies to consider all three criteria for performance, and is generally considered to have raised the bar in terms of CSR in Southern Africa.

Finally, the mainstreaming of CSR reporting to SMEs seems like a positive and inevitable trend. There are simply too many advantages to smaller firms to leave sustainability reporting to multinationals. In parallel, sustainability and CSR information will increasingly be presented with financial information, rather than in a separate report. In an ideal world, it will be prepared with the same rigour, and given the same importance within firms.

Conclusion

We have seen how CSR has emerged as a discipline from the industrial revolution through to the growth of the modern, global world of business. It is clear that the range of responsibilities for which companies are being held responsible is widening, and that legal form is no barrier to responsibilities, as the various supply chain scandals have shown. Soft codes and industry codes of conduct, from the Kimberly Process for diamonds to the Harkin–Engel Protocol for cocoa are becoming the norm. Reporting has become more formalised, and is likely to be more widespread in coming years. SMEs have, to a large extent, yet to get to grips with the field of CSR and sustainability, but this too is changing.

---

[80] See www.jse.co.za/About-Us/SRI/Introduction_to_SRI_Index.aspx; last accessed 16 April 2012.

CSR is still evolving, and remains a contested discipline. It has already had enormous impact on how business is done and, despite its many failings and limitations, that impact overall has been positive. The next 20 years should see CSR mainstreamed into business strategy, improving the relationship between business and society, for the benefit of all.

...

And if the world were black or white entirely
And all the charts were plain
Instead of a mad weir of tigerish waters,
A prism of delight and pain,
We might be surer where we wished to go
Or again we might be merely
Bored but in brute reality there is no
Road that is right entirely.

...

"Entirely"
Louis MacNeice

Part II

The Practice – Irish Experiences of CSR

Introduction to Part II

In this part, founders, CEOs and senior executives of eight Irish businesses talk about what CSR means for them, and what is being done within their firms. Interviewed in 2011, at a time when most of them were going through rapid change and struggling with economic recession, their stories make up an interesting snapshot of what CSR means to Irish businesses in the post 'Celtic Tiger' years.

In each case, the interviews were semi-structured, covering more or less the same ground. Each transcript was then edited into a first-person narrative, so that the story is told directly by the entrepreneur. For ease of reading, the accounts are broken into topics, dealing, for example, with what CSR means to the business, the relevance or otherwise of CSR standards and external reporting, etc. The result is a collection of business people telling their own experiences of how they deal with CSR, what it means for them and where they see it evolving.

The businesses featured are varied and comprise:

- a printing company operating from a village in the west of Ireland;
- a titanium mining plc operating in Mozambique;
- a long-established city bookshop;
- an island coffee shop and surf school;
- a newly-established two-person HR consultancy;
- a public sports centre in Northern Ireland;
- a family-run hotel in rural Limerick; and
- a company supplying school lunches all over Ireland.

Despite this diversity, there are a lot of common experiences, and the ways in which the firms grapple with CSR issues are remarkably similar.

Common themes that emerge include the importance of leaders in setting the ethos of the firm, and the significance of the personal values of the founder or the directors. Recruitment and probation periods are also seen as very important in ensuring that the ethos permeates the firm as a whole. Honesty and transparency is a common theme, particularly in terms of pricing or in the business's dealings with the community. Most of the entrepreneurs are reluctant to beat their own drum when it comes to CSR, and this is coupled with a general lack of awareness on how CSR could be reported to external stakeholders, as discussed in **Chapter 6**.

Many of the owners and managers interviewed do not tend to use the term corporate social responsibility to describe what they do, although, on reflection, they can see that it fits. A strong sense comes through most of the accounts of wanting to run the business in a particular way that is often linked to the owners' sense of identity and personal values, reflecting the virtue-based ethics approach mentioned in **Exhibit 2**. This can be called the '**second nature**' quality of many of the CSR initiatives in smaller firms. They do things in a particular way because it is instinctive, or in tune with their own values, rather than because a separate moral case or business case has been made for this way of doing business. The downside is that the CSR initiatives may be undervalued, and certainly under-reported. The upside is that smaller firms, because their CSR derives from a genuine ethos, generally achieve a more integrated embodiment of their CSR activities. It is this sincerity that larger firms find challenging. There is also a common focus on the **long-term** in smaller firms, especially in taking a view on the business payback from short-term costs associated with particular ways of operating. Finally, there is a common theme of **respect**, which encompasses respect for staff, customers and the community.

Each of the accounts is preceded by some background to the business, and more detail on each of the firms is available on the websites listed. The generosity of the eight individuals in giving their time and sharing their experiences was remarkable and, together, they have created a fascinating picture of CSR in Ireland.

Case A

The Printer

KPS Colourprint is a commercial printing company operating from large, modern premises just outside the village of Knock, County Mayo. The company prints a wide range of products, including magazines, books, stationery, annual reports, inserts and memoriam cards. They use very advanced technology, and all finishing is completed in-house, which speeds the turnaround time on orders and gives the company more control over quality.

The company was formed in 1994 by Brendan Salmon, then in his early thirties, and with 13 years' experience in the printing industry. Brendan operates the company with a strong ethos of respect for his employees, and an egalitarian attitude to relationships within the workplace.He founded the company in a garage beside his home, and two years later, leased a factory in Knock, County Mayo, which he bought outright in 1999. In 2002, the company invested heavily in state-of-the-art equipment, enabling them to expand. Five years later, the company moved to a purpose-built facility outside the village of Knock, where it now employs between 14 and 20 people. For more detail on the company, visit www.kpscolourprint.com.

I spoke to CEO and founder, Brendan Salmon, in 2011, and he began by discussing the recession.

On the Recession

In 2009, things got tight. In 2010, things got tighter, and now, in 2011, things are even tighter again. But we keep working with our bankers and with the people we have leased from. We've arranged for payment holidays and for restructuring of leases because it's unfair to pay for equipment on a full-time basis when they're only on four days' production. We just try to ride the recession out like that. At peak times, we could have maybe 20 people working here; at the moment I think there are 13 or 14. We have a very nice team of part-time people as well, because the market is so volatile. It's like a feast or a famine. August is always a quiet month.

The memoriam card business needs a different set of skills, listening skills and so on. I have a few girls here working with me who are very good at that, and I let them handle all of that part of the business. Sometimes, people find it hard to choose, and they need someone to encourage and help them. It's something I set up a few years ago as a distinct part of the business. It runs as a nice filler in between the more commercial jobs you might have on hand, because it means we can have a bigger team of people. That's good for us – it gives us flexibility. It means we can pull people from one job into another when we need to.

What CSR Means in the Business

I always wanted to run the business by concentrating on quality. We don't print everything, and what we do print, we try to do it right. We can't work for nothing. We choose to work for people who respect a good product, people who know that they may pay a bit more for a quality product.

Apart from our quality, we have the reputation for delivering on time. We are always very honest with our customers. If it's a two-day turnaround, we'll say it is a two-day turnaround. We treat their job like a baby, and make sure it's out there on time. That reputation is very important.

A lot of companies are driven by market share, turnover. I'm not. I look more at profitability. Turnover to me is not everything. In this climate, if I can survive the recession and pay my employees, that's enough. So, our customers, and being honest with them, that's an important part of CSR for me.

The employees are the backbone of the business. It gives me a lot of job satisfaction to know that, on a Friday evening, I can bring the lads to the pub, and there are no issues. We can have a pint or play a game of football together, or a game of darts. That's a good reflection on the company, to see the MD and the employees out socialising together. Everybody can see that there are no hidden problems here: all the staff are happy, and they all have a few bob in their pocket. That's a big thing in a small place like this.

It's better for all of us. When you try to have a good understanding of a new worker, after a short while, you know whether you can work with this guy or not, whether or not he's suitable for the industry. It's not everybody that's suitable for this sort of industry. You know that quickly from their ability and their care in handling equipment and machines, whether they are good, careful people or not. That's part of the recruitment and probation system we have in place. The result is that we have a good team of people here. Some people are with me 9 or 10 years, and they know that I will look after them.

It's also very satisfying to me that there's no tension. There are sometimes issues between employees themselves that you have to iron out. And, sometimes, there is no ironing out, you just keep them apart. That hasn't happened very often, but it's easier to address these things sooner rather than later. It definitely suits me better to run my business like that.

On the Usefulness of External Standards

Sustainability and environment issues are more or less dealt with by our certification by external boards or bodies. They cover environmental issues like noise, recycling material, the chain of certification for the materials we use. We're now members of the Forest Stewardship Council[81] and the Programme for the Endorsement of Forest Certification.[82] These are the best sustainable forestry chain of custody certification bodies, so all the environmental issues are taken care of through there.

It's good to have those standards. They also enable us to get our employees trained up. It makes them aware, say, of the consequences of throwing a can of coke into a bag of paper. There are penalties for that sort of thing, so the standards are very useful. We have had them in place here for years, especially for recycling materials like cardboard or office material like toner cartridges, printers, computer screens, etc. That's a major saving rather than a cost. It makes everyone that bit more responsible.

These external standards are the same as standards that I've always had in my own mind. I've visited nearly every printing house in the country, and it's easy to see how things are wasted. You can see the attitude of people and how they waste good material and let down customers on quality issues. These are things that could be easily improved on, for the benefit of the business. You get educated in business if you keep your eyes open. I was always led by the mistakes I've seen in other companies, as well as the external standards.

Making CSR Part of the Ethos

It doesn't cost anything to keep a place tidy, but if it gets into a mess, it will be a huge cost then to restore it. I make sure this place is cleaned, hoovered

---

[81] www.fsc.org.

[82] www.pefc.org.

and mopped every Friday evening. It's not just health and safety; it creates a better working environment.

So, when I start off new employees here, I tell them: "This is what happens on Friday evening – everything has to be cleaned. This is your job – there's the brush." I have a great relationship with the guys in the store, the girls in the office, and so on. They're working *with* me as opposed to working for me, which is very important. And it's a source of satisfaction to me, because I have a relationship with the employees. At the end of the day, we're all just human beings. Whether or not they're working for me, we're all working for KPS Colourprint.

It's about respect, which is the same thing we have here with all the employees. I respect them, and they know it, so then they have the same attitude to the customers. They treat them the same way as I would. Now the customers know that in my absence they can deal with any one of my employees, and they will be looked after.

The Origins of the Firm's Ethos

The ethos here comes very much from my own values: respect, honesty, doing the job right. I'm not thinking yet about changes in leadership or succession or anything like that. There's no way for me to start thinking about that in this recession. I just have to improve the efficiencies of everybody so that the company itself can be more efficient to give the customers better value, because they are all shopping around. We all work together here; it's all a win–win, and my ultimate aim is to provide security for the employees that I have.

The Advantages of CSR, and the Future

We're always willing to learn more, and watch other companies and see how they're behaving or trading. We learn from their mistakes. We try very hard to look after our customers, even those who might only come back to you once or maybe twice a year. Now that we're in a recession, that's even more important. Customers have to feel as if they're being cared for. If you look after people, they will always come back to you. They might stray one day, but they'll always come back the next, and they'll stay with you then. We just show appreciation to the customer, and let them know that we are thankful for their business.

That ethos is really important, but I don't put it on our website because I don't think it's really of relevance to our customers. It's just how we run the business internally. Every company has its own way of doing things. I hear of problems in other companies, and a lot of it seems to be about power and control. If the leader is too focussed on that, it creates ill feeling among the workers, and then the company has to employ more people to carry out quality assurance work. A lot of these costs could easily be eliminated if the management had a slightly better understanding of employees.

We don't need to look down on others; whether I'm the boss or you're the boss, we're all here to get a job done. My wages are not phenomenally better than his or hers. At the end of the day, there should always be respect between people in the company, and that creates the atmosphere we all want in a workplace. We're all human beings.

It is clear that the way in which KPS operates comes from Brendan's own personal ethos. Because it is sincere in that way, it feeds into all aspects of the business seamlessly, and is visible in the high standard of attention paid to customers, the fostering of a good work–life balance for employees, the reduction in waste, etc.

The business was started with a clear vision of what sort of company it would be. External CSR and environmental standards are seen as something that can be used to implement this vision, rather than a constraint. It is interesting that the affiliation with the Forest Stewardship Council and the Programme for the Endorsement of Forest Certification is clearly seen as a benefit rather than a cost to the business.

The company does not currently report on its CSR or environmental policies, partly because they are largely unarticulated, and partly because no added value is seen in reporting. However, the company could easily report using the GRI framework (discussed in **Chapter 5**) and, in doing so, would be able to get into the supply chains of and win contracts from large firms that are seeking to have more green, environmentally-friendly production. As CSR reporting and CSR auditing of the supply chain by Irish businesses becomes more widespread, it is likely that business-to-business (B2B) operations such as KPS Colourprint will begin to see the strategic advantages of CSR reporting.

Case B

The Mine

Kenmare Resources, established in 1972, is an Irish mining company quoted on the London and Irish Stock Exchanges. It is a member of the FTSE 250 Index, and the company's main activity is a heavy minerals mine at Moma in Northern Mozambique, where it employs over 700 people. The mine produces titanium used in paints, paper and plastic, and zircon used in ceramic tile and steel production. Construction of the mine began in 2004. Prior to that, Kenmare operated the Ancuabe Graphite Mine in Mozambique. The company also holds a small number of exploration licences in Ireland. At 30 June 2011, the total assets of the company were in excess of $830 billion.

Kenmare reports its CSR activities externally, integrating a responsibility statement with the company's annual and interim financial statements. There is also a significant section on their website devoted to describing their CSR activities, which centre on the community surrounding the Moma Mine. The company has won several awards for its CSR programme. See www.kenmareresources.com for more details.

I spoke to the company's Financial Controller, Deirdre Corcoran, and she began by discussing why CSR matters to Kenmare.

Why CSR Matters to Kenmare

Corporate Social Responsibility is a key aspect of business for the Board of Directors. We devote a lot of time and focus to our responsibilities. We have a long-established relationship with the communities in the area where we operate, and to further our responsibilities, we established a Development Association in 2004. That was at a time when we were beginning the construction of the mine that we're currently operating. We were conscious of the fact that construction was going to bring a change in the dynamic of the area. There was going to be an influx of construction workers initially and, subsequently, employees into the area. We wanted to work with local communities to ensure that change was managed effectively, and that the heads of those communities were involved. It was important to ensure that it was done responsibly in a way that would minimise any negative impacts, and increase the benefits that could be attributable to the communities.

So, the Development Association was established in 2004, principally with the objective of maximising the economic gain that could be gained for the community. We appreciated that there would be services that needed to be provided; for example, food and supplies would need to be brought in. If these could be supplied locally, if we could work with the local community to develop business ideas and develop businesses to supply the mine and other markets for their local produce, then there would be a benefit for everybody.

How CSR is Implemented

One of the initial projects was vegetable production. We provided training to local farmers in growing food that would supply the mine. Work has evolved since then in terms of other supply businesses. We have an egg production project. We also have a fish project where we work with the local fishermen. Previously, they didn't have very good methods of preserving fish; they'd catch them, but they didn't have cooling systems or coolers. Within a number of hours, in the heat of the day in Mozambique, the fish would have gone off. We supplied cooler boxes, and they now have the ability to chill the fish, which extends the shelf life of the fish. A salt production business has also commenced ... A lot of the measures are relatively simple, but they mean that there is a greater ability for the local people to sell produce.

The market for locally produced food in some areas is principally the mine, but a market among nearby villages has also evolved. For example, with the eggs produced, a percentage is sold to the mine, but an increasing percentage is sold to local communities. We've worked with groups to establish businesses and to provide business training in managing these businesses, in accessing markets and in accessing raw materials or other inputs required for their business, which are key to the sustainability of their operation. We provide them with the skills to be able to access Nampula, which is the nearest town about a four to five-hour drive away. Now, they cooperatively arrange transport. When they go, they get the materials they need, and when the trip is being arranged, they bring produce to the market as well, and to markets along the way.

The Development Association, in conjunction with the community through consultation, has developed a five-year strategic plan to respond to the needs of the community. Health was identified as a key issue. Earlier, the Association had done a lot of work in education – on the construction of schools and provision of materials and school furniture. That has helped improve access to education in the community. Health was now identified as a priority area.

On Partnering

We have been working collaboratively with the Ministry of Health in Mozambique to see how we could address the situation. HIV education and awareness training is something that we have been involved in from the start. We were aware that one of the potential negative impacts on the community of the mine could be an increase in HIV/Aids. In 2004, one of the starter programs we had was a HIV-awareness program, for both the mine and local communities. Malaria is another key health concern. There are not that many health centres around. There are some health posts, but they are poorly equipped. The nearest health clinic is about a 10-kilometre walk away. For a lot of the people who don't have transport and are sick, they just can't travel this distance.

To address this issue, the Association agreed to the construction of a health clinic, which would be staffed and operated by the Ministry of Health. One of the key concerns for us is sustainability. We needed a commitment from the Ministry that it would be staffed and funded when it is complete. We've now got that commitment, and we started construction of the clinic at the start of 2011. It is scheduled to be operational in 2012. That will give access to a higher level of healthcare service to the local communities.

In the meantime, the Association supports a mobile clinic service in the area. This consists of a doctor and dentist team who come in every two weeks, visit the local health posts that already exist, in a range of about eight to 10 villages up to a 15 to 20 kilometre radius from the mine. The mobile clinic team work with the health staff employed by the Ministry of Health, providing them with further training and up-skilling them so that skills are retained within the area, and there is greater outreach to the local communities. They also train community volunteers, who provide basic first aid and health care.

We have been fortunate to be able to link up with a Danish NGO based in Nampula comprising a doctor and dentist and their teams. They have a specific interest in doing this. They previously had a similar service in Australia and wanted to expand into Mozambique. It fitted with our wish to provide improved health services in the community. We arrange for them to fly in every two weeks, providing them with logistical support to get around, as well as with food and accommodation when they are in the area.

The Association also bought an ambulance for the community, so if there are patients that need further care, we can arrange for that to happen. The project is funded by Kenmare and by one of our project lenders, who also provides funding for technical assistance and capacity building on other programmes.

Malaria prevention is an area on which we are also focused. While we've provided malaria nets to local communities for a long period of time, there's still a high rate of malaria in the area, so we sought permission from the Ministry of Health to fund a spraying programme to help reduce the existence of malaria. We have managed to successfully secure the authority to do this, and the spraying programme has now been carried out. These are the key areas of healthcare focus for the Association.

We have a close relationship with the people in Irish Aid in both Mozambique and Dublin. They are very aware of what we do. The way they work, certainly in Mozambique, is that they are allocated various provinces to work in. They work in two different provinces, not where we work, which is Nampula province. Therefore, in terms of their ability to work with our projects, they're restricted, but we … sought advice from them when we set up the Association. We are one of the few Irish companies operating in Mozambique. We keep them informed of our operations. If there is anything they can assist us with, we notify them.

On Consultation

More broadly in terms of Kenmare and its CSR, the Development Association is one aspect of how we manage that. Keeping local communities informed of what we do as a business is something that we consider to be very important. We have bi-monthly meetings, where representatives of those communities come and are given an update as to what we are doing as a business, what affects them in terms of employment of people from the locality, and other issues. And we hear what issues they have. If they have concerns as to how we are running the business or how it's impacted on them, we listen to those concerns, and we address them with feedback in the next bi-monthly meeting.

That interaction has worked well for us, since we've started the construction of the mine in 2004, and through the period of operation. Prior to that, we were running an exploration camp, which was a much smaller scale operation but, again, sought to involve the local communities and keep them informed regarding operations. In general, the community has responded favourably to the mine and how we are managing it. We're there as their guests if you like. We have made a business that has transformed the landscape of the area. It's important that they are involved.

On Reporting of CSR

This approach is driven from the top down. The Kenmare Board are very focused on this as an area, and feel it's important to how we run the business. It's engrained in the organisation, from the Board down to senior management and all mine personnel. To make that happen, we have regular reporting requirements. For instance, at the Association, we have weekly reports on projects, community interaction, etc. We have similar reports at corporate level. In every report that's generated from the mine, equally as important as the production data are the community, environmental and safety statistics. It's the first part of any report, and, again, the fact that we require this drives its importance. We have regular visits from directors and senior management to the mine. For each of those visits, there will be an element of monitoring – going out to meet with the local representatives in the communities. As a business, it is given equal importance.

The Development Association reports to us on an annual basis and provides frequent reports to all funders of the Association. Kenmare's annual report contains a CSR section where we outline what we do in terms of environmental and community work. We do this for stakeholders in the business generally, and for shareholders or people who have provided finance to the organisation or are involved in any way in the business. I think it is important that we put forward what we are doing and the values we hold as a company. Our investors, for instance, might have criteria that they consider important for investment. Without knowing what we do, they can't make an investment decision.

Challenges

There have been challenges. Anything we fund has to have a sustainability aspect to it, and there are a lot of requests from the communities we work in. What we have done over the last number of years is give the opportunity to the communities to put ideas forward to the Development Association. We are very conscious in running any project that there are only a certain number of beneficiaries we can work with. That leaves a level of inequality in the community because some people get a financial benefit, while their neighbour may not.

On the whole, however, it all feeds down into the communities. If there is more money to spend, the benefit is widespread. Selecting the right beneficiaries, the ones most in need, the ones who can manage it the best, not just the most influential – that is very important. Sometimes, we have let the community select a dozen or 10 beneficiaries on a project. We have to ensure that we assist the beneficiaries most in need in the community. This is principally women, by virtue of the fact that the wealth passes around. It's important … that there is an awareness of the need to be involved and to ensure the funding is done right and in keeping with the objectives of the Association.

My favourite initiative is the healthcare project. The long-term benefits of that program are significant for a community that had very poor access to healthcare. I think that program, through the mobile clinic, malaria programs, HIV program and construction of the health clinic, has had, and will continue to have, a big impact. With improved healthcare, the other initiatives that we have will work better. Fundamentally, if people have good health, then they have more of an ability to continue in school, get an education, set up business and work, and improve their quality of life and move out of the poverty trap. That gives them an ability to have a good lifestyle. I think that is core to everything else. If there is poor health, short life expectancy and illness in the area, it is very difficult for development to take place in that community.

Kenmare hope to be operational at Moma for the long term, so getting it right from the beginning is very important. We strive not to have a dependency established between us and the community. Whatever initiatives are there, once they are established, the less involvement from us the better. The hairdressing business and the bakery are creating employment. There is an influx of people to the area. Even without the mine, you would hope the community that has developed would be there regardless because it has established its own businesses and can maintain itself in the long term.

On the Future

I think that as we evolve and grow as a business, and expand further in the area, it will become even more critical that we involve the communities in what we are doing in the areas we work in, and that we minimise any negative consequences. It is difficult to have an influx of people into the area without some negative change. The lesson we have learned is to continue to strive for improvement all the time. We need to constantly assess any risk there is to the community and to eliminate that risk in all aspects of the business.

What we see as the future, I think, is continuing to prioritise the local community, continuing to manage the business responsibly and continuing to involve communities. It's important as we grow not to let those standards slip and, where possible, to enhance them.

In commencing operations in a country beset by poverty, poor health, lack of education and weak infrastructure, Kenmare faced particular challenges in implementing a CSR policy. Mining as an industry faces particular challenges, especially in the areas of the environment and of health and safety. This was compounded by the fact that they were operating in a developing country, so the level of support and implementation from a government with limited resources would not equate to that obtainable in the EU, for instance.

Despite this, the company has delivered very positive initiatives to the community surrounding the mine. Because of the limitations of the government locally, they have taken on a wide range of issues that would not have been seen as the company's problem otherwise. For example, if they were operating in their home country of Ireland, they would not have been likely to take on the health of the local population, or the provision of transport to local traders as responsibilities. This is a good illustration of the sort of geographical differences in CSR standards referred to in **Exhibit 12**.

The interaction with the local community is described in terms of mutual respect, echoing a key theme of KPS Colourprint. The role of reporting, both external and internal, is also interesting. The company uses internal reporting as a way of driving the ethos throughout the workforce. As a larger plc, they also see the value of reporting externally, linking it to the requirements of investors and other stakeholders. The malaria project is a solid example of partnering (as described in **Chapter 3**).

Also of interest is the way in which Deirdre describes the company's involvement in Mozambique as being long term, linking this directly to their approach to CSR:

"Kenmare hope to be operational at Moma for the long term, so getting it right from the beginning is very important".

This illustrates directly the link described in **Chapter 4** between sustainability and a long-term view.

Case C

The Bookshop

O'Mahony's Bookshop is a family-run business, which has traded from its landmark premises on the main street of Limerick City for over a hundred years. The business was started in 1902 by J.P. O'Mahony, grandfather of the current owners, in a premises of 450 square feet, selling books, leather goods, religious goods and stationery. His grandsons, Frank and David, became the third generation to run the business when they inherited a half-share in the business following the death of their father (the other half-share at the time going to their mother). The brothers have received several industry awards, and both are former Presidents of the Irish Booksellers' Association.

As well as the flagship premises on O'Connell Street in Limerick, the company operates retail branches at the University of Limerick, in Ennis and in Tralee. The company's online presence (at www.omahonys .ie) is growing rapidly. O'Mahony's also has a non-retail business in Cork and a distribution warehouse on the Dock Road in Limerick. The main shop in Limerick City is the largest bookshop in the city, and one of the oldest retail outlets in the region. In total, the company has 25,000 square feet of retail space, and employs 100 people.

I spoke to David O'Mahony, and he began by discussing how he and his brother came into the business.

On Family Succession

Normally, what you hear about family businesses is that the first generation makes it, the second generation builds it, and the third generation destroys it. We've been fortunate in that we're only on the third generation, although the family is in business in total for over 100 years. You might normally expect four generations in that time. My dad started in 1916, and worked in the business until he died in 1979. [My brother] Frank went into the business in

1973 after taking a degree in Economics from UCD. I graduated from the University of Limerick in 1977 with a degree in Business Studies, and joined the business the following year. After my father died, my brother and I received between us a half-share in the business, and my mother retained the other half. Later, she divested herself of her share to us equally. So, it was a very specific situation where we were equal partners. Not 49:51, but 50:50. The logic of that was that, well, we *had* to agree. It was a very wise move.

What CSR means to O'Mahony's

For us, CSR means a lot of different things. There's a strong community aspect to it, because we are Limerick-based, and we have that longevity as a business, so people expect things of us. We are part of the history of the city. Maybe that expectation from the public has its origins in that we have always had a socially responsible way of doing business. Good business means understanding your customer and understanding your community, and responding to their demands, be they commercially driven or non-commercially driven. You'd like to think that all your actions would be more than just financially based. Limerick is very important to us. It's very important to me, personally, perhaps because it's an area that I have been involved in, and maybe because Limerick has had its own difficulties. We need to step up and, indeed, lots of traders need to step up, to try and get recognition for a city that is much maligned.

We do a lot of work with libraries also. Twenty years ago we were dealing with nearly every library in the country, from Cork to Galway to Donegal, maybe less so in Dublin or in Cork, but lots of the small libraries. That's one of those things, supplying them with some books, where you'd say, 'OK, it's the right thing to do. It's not making us a fortune but it's the right thing to do.' We did a large renovation about 15 years ago, and we realised that we had a very formidable shop. We had very good staff. We really wanted to make a song and dance about it, and we did, happily. Now ours is the shop that librarians from the four corners of Ireland come to visit. They travel to Limerick to pull stock from the shelves. Before we publicised ourselves, they wouldn't dream of doing that. They'd say: 'What do you mean? Haven't we enough bookshops in Dublin? Or Cork?' They didn't – believe it or not, and I'm not blowing my own trumpet here – they didn't have a stockholding bookshop like O'Mahony's in those cities. They had Eason's and Waterstone's, which is gone now, and so on, but they were not necessarily as interested in libraries as we were.

We always had a close association with the education market: primary, secondary and, now, tertiary. We work very hard on relationships; it could be a two-teacher primary school, a 20-teacher primary school, or a 50-teacher secondary school, but each relationship is equally important to us. Because parents were spending a lot of money buying school books in our shops, they would tend to think that O' Mahony's owed them something in return. They wanted something back and we understood that. So, maybe it arose from that kind of expectation, but we always knew that we had to provide a bit of sponsorship here and there. We had to give support to the parents' groups if they were doing fashion shows or things like that. That happens through the normal course of business, but it was the relationship that we had and the way we understood their expectations that started it.

As the business grew, we created employment opportunities – temporary work during the summer, placements during work experience weeks in schools ... Some of those students then go onto teacher training colleges and become the teachers of the future. That all helps to propagate the name of the O'Mahony business. It's difficult to isolate any one thing we do as purely altruistic, but I think it's a whole collection of little pieces that end up making the case.

On the Origin of the Business's Ethos

Why we run our business like we do could be down to the influence of our parents. Both of them were very good, Christian people, with a moral perspective. We might not have inherited all their wonderful beliefs, but certainly the philosophy of engaging with the community came down the generations to us. Engaging and being responsible is just something we do naturally.

When you have a business with a lot of people in it, you have to put your own values out there, and let them be seen. The ethos of the organisation as a whole has to come from the top down, and it has to go right down through the organisation. You'd like to think that the people you empower in positions of responsibility in the company engender all the values that you have. It has to go all the way down to the guy sweeping out the store and taking in the goods from the back – respect, communication and recognition.

On Challenges

I don't mean to say we haven't made mistakes in the past. Certainly, however, we would have been aiming for this way of doing business when we started back in the 1970s, and even from the sidelines before we engaged in the business. When we started, we saw that most people that worked for and represented O'Mahony's had very long service with the company. There were two directors there, and when they retired, each had in the region of 40 years' service. A good number of the employees back then would have had 20 or 30 years' service. It's interesting to look at the difference: in the 1950s and 60s, customer service and recognition were very important. It used to be noted that we had a very low staff turnover; and that was always seen as an indicator of how well a business was performing. In fact, our staff turnover was so low that it was practically static, which created its own problems. When we 'young bucks' went in to the business, we thought we needed some more staff turnover to keep people on their toes and to energise. Then, over a period, that did happen, as some of the older employees who had been magnificent in helping to grow the business became less dominant. By then, we had younger people working here, just as enthusiastic, but with different views, different reading habits. (With a bookshop, you have to ensure that your people do a reasonable bit of reading.)

Staff are so important. You have to ensure we are employing the right people. You know reasonably quickly when you meet someone; you can sense their enthusiasm. We have been very fortunate. Certainly, one thing that would set us aside from other bookshops is the customer reaction to our staff. While my brother and I give direction and feedback, they're the people carrying it out. I think you have to give them space.

Before we joined the business, things were very autocratic. Now, I think the power is a little bit more devolved. You must empower people. If they make a mistake, they make a mistake, and you hope that they learn, and it won't be catastrophic. You hold up your hand to the customer and say: "I'm sorry, we made a mistake. I apologise." And, of course, the staff member apologises too, and hopefully we learn.

On Reporting about CSR

It's only when we really think about it and put all the things together that we realise that, gosh, there's a lot more going on than we would have probably realised. Things we do in the CSR area are happening in an ad-hoc way, rather than in a concerted, policy-driven way.

You know, the large multinationals might pay lip-service to corporate social responsibility and have it embedded in their strategy, but actually, a lot of what we do and the way in which we do it is because of the way we were brought up. This is continuing the ethos and the community aspect of our business. I wouldn't have thought it was any big deal, but when you put it altogether you say: "Oh yeah, well that's a lot more than I would have thought." We don't advertise our CSR initiatives and, sometimes, people have found out afterwards what we do, and have said: "I never knew O'Mahony's did this or that." Perhaps if they'd known about it beforehand, we could have developed a better relationship with them. So, we could put a section on our website, perhaps. Perhaps we should wave our flag a little bit more.

It is interesting that when David is searching for examples of O'Mahony's CSR, he comments:

> "It's difficult to isolate any one thing we do as purely altruistic, but I think it's a whole collection of little pieces that end up making the case."

This is a representative statement of what CSR means for many small firms. It is entirely appropriate that the initiatives are not totally altruistic, because as we have seen, particularly at **Exhibit 16** in **Chapter 8**, pure altruism is not necessary for a business to embody corporate social responsibility.

This is a good example of the 'second nature' quality of CSR found in many SMEs referred to earlier in the introduction to Part II. O'Mahony's is a beautiful shop, and the reaction of the public to the staff, as described by David, is very tangible.

The value of external reporting is beginning to be visible to O'Mahony's, particularly once there has been some reflection on what CSR means to them. It would not be a big step for this business to take on GRI-compliant reporting.

The company also has an interesting relationship with the community. Unlike Kenmare, which arrived in Mozambique and set about assessing the needs of the community, O'Mahony's is already an integral part of the history of Limerick City. This closeness is both a strength and a burden, as illustrated by the expectations of the business from the public and, particularly, from parents and schools.

Case D

The Coffee Shop and Surf School

Blackfield Clothing and Surf School is a family-run coffee shop and surf school operating in the beautiful surroundings of Achill Island, County Mayo. The company also designs and makes a unique range of fleece clothing, sold in their surf shop, online and to shops all over Ireland. All the fleece clothes are Irish made.

The company was founded by computer scientist Gerry Brannigan and his wife Sabine, largely as a lifestyle choice, from a desire to live and work in Achill. The island, the largest off the coast of Ireland, is connected to the mainland by a bridge. It is heavily dependent on tourism, although the summer season is very short. There is an increasing move to extend the season by focusing on outdoor pursuits, particularly running, surfing and cycling.

See www.blackfield.com for more details.

I spoke to founder, Gerry Brannigan, and he began by talking about what CSR meant to him.

What CSR Means to Blackfield

Thinking about what CSR means to us, there are certain examples that come to mind. There's an interesting movement happening in Ireland and worldwide at the moment called 'HelpX'.[83] This is a website that places people who are looking for work in businesses that will accommodate them, without paying them. A little like WWOOF[84] for organic farms. The problem with it is that if you visit a lot of the seasonal business establishments in any tourist area, you'll find people working there that are not from the community, who wouldn't know very much about the area and, most importantly, who are not

---

[83] See www.helpx.net.
[84] Worldwide Opportunities on Organic Farms; see www.wwoof.org.

getting paid. They are just getting their board and food for the course of maybe six weeks over that busy term in the summer. Now, we've always employed local people, both seasonally and fulltime.

It's not that I feel a responsibility to be an employer, to employ people. No business should have that as their *raison d'être*. But, since we do have to employ people, we would like to do it from within the community, and have always done. We have kids that are going to college, and we know they need the money. Or, when we employ local people, we know this is helping their everyday needs. We could have decided to move into the HelpX system, to have people working here who would cost us far less. Also, they're paid as almost a barter, or in kind, so they are obviously out of the exchequer or Revenue net. There's nothing going back into the system for their work, so there's probably a lot more bottom line coming down to the business as a result of it. We chose not to do that.

There's the wider exchequer benefit of employing and paying people from the local community. That's part of CSR for us as well. We've never shirked the tax responsibility that we have. We tried to lower our bills, of course, as every business does, but we've always felt that, yes, there's a contribution to be made there because the country does need money to keep it going.

Otherwise, we would look carefully at what we sell. For instance, we sell Illy coffee here. Fairtrade is obviously a massive issue, but Illy coffee is not part of that movement. However, we have satisfied ourselves about what they do. Illy have deliberately stepped outside of that movement, but they would still see themselves as a fair trade producer of coffee. That's important, because it can be a hugely exploitative field. When we look at our sugars, we would try to use Fairtrade when we can.

On Challenges

Not using HelpX obviously has a cost as an employer. There is a benefit as well. In this case, the benefit is a direct knock-on one, that someone in the community will find it that little bit easier for their kid to go to college. I don't really know if I'd say the community is a stakeholder in the business, but we can certainly make a difference to our direct community by employing someone locally rather than bringing in someone for free.

For the other things we sell in the shop, we have always tried to look carefully at what we sell, but there is a balance. At one stage, we were, if anything, too ethical or too green. It's difficult to be like that nowadays. We found that when we stocked organic clothing, for instance, we just couldn't sell it. So, we've had to compromise on that. The planet will have to take some sort of a hit there. We would be very aware of where we're buying our stock, though, and the processes that go into making a lot of what we offer. Maybe, instead of buying organic cotton, we might choose producers that are using dyes that may be approved to be less damaging. Like everything else, it's a diminishing effect rather than a zero effect. We also know that there are certain products that we get from certain companies and goodness knows where they come from. That's just the way it is.

Still, there are certainly things we wouldn't sell. If somebody came to us and said: "Look, we know for sure that this is being made in a sweatshop in India," then we would say, "We can't touch that." We have worked with Fair-trade companies sourcing jewellery especially because that's quite a good product for Fairtrade. There's lots of it going around, and it's all well-priced. Most of the jewellery that we had in would have come from sources like that.

On Standards and Reporting

We don't highlight our purchasing policy in the shop. We would have in the past, but I don't think it's a huge selling point. Price and style are what people are looking for here. If they can salve their conscience at the same time, then that's all well and good, but I don't think it's a purchasing decision for an awful lot of people.

We look at standards, but we don't report them on our website. We'd love to, but we don't, probably because of constraints on our time more than anything else. We would have to write up all the standards on the website, and then, next year, we'd have to do the same again. Certainly in the surf school, we would work within every single standard that's required of us, and more. We aim to operate an efficient and a good, safe, reputable school. There are a couple of things with the surf school that are interesting. For instance, at some stage, we do take the kids and make them clean the stretch of beach that we use. It's not their favourite part of the Surf School, but we do it with most of them. We do it because we're all using the beach, and we want to leave it pristine. There's education in doing that too. We try to educate them as much as possible about the environment that they're in because it's amazing the lack of knowledge that's out there.

On the Future and the Origins of the Business's Ethos

These things are personal. It goes back to the reason why we're here in the first place. We are very aware of the issues that are involved in terms of the environment, and also human rights, and so on. For me, that's just what it means to be a relatively decent human being. We have to respect all the principles – profit, planet, people. We would certainly see ourselves as having to make a profit, but we don't see ourselves as having to destroy anything in order to do it. I think that's a very simple principle that we try to live by.

If we sold the business, this whole ethos could disappear really fast, couldn't it? If our kids were to take it over, they would have the same sense as ourselves because they spend a lot of time here. Certainly, the environmental aspect, they're into that. This is where they live, so they don't want to muck it up. They'd be very aware of issues like that, and would continue what we're doing in the same way. If we sold the business to somebody else, though, would it be a deal breaker if they said: "We're going to buy all the stuff in from China?" I'd hardly think so. It would be nice if our ethos continued, because it would all be set up for the new owners, to some degree. I guess if you're trying to get out of your business, you'd hope that someone would come in and carry it on the way you wanted. And maybe it would be silly of them not to.

More and more, we work with other businesses, this being an island, but not as much as you'd think. There's not an awful lot that we can do, really. Certainly in terms of the outdoor stuff, we would work with some of the hotels and B&Bs, and some of the other facility providers, and I'm involved in Achill Tourism as well.

Whatever we do, we wouldn't necessarily call it CSR. It would just be integrated into our everyday way of going about our business. It's our living moving into our work, I guess. It's the influence of the individual. If you have an interest in keeping the environment in any kind of a shape, then that automatically transfers into the business.

This is a particularly reflective account. Clearly, Gerry has thought a lot about the role of the business on the island, and in the world, and what its responsibilities might be. He does not, for example, see employing people as an obligation, although they have made a conscious decision to avoid HelpX and instead employ local people where possible to work seasonally in the shop. He is thoughtful about what options are open to the company, given that organic cotton is not a good seller in their market.

This reflection has led Gerry to identify a wider range of possible CSR issues than most other entrepreneurs. He mentions the importance of paying a fair share of tax, for instance, and is the only respondent to mention human rights. He also sees the environment in a wider context than simply waste reduction. The link to the local community for Blackfield is seen in this context – the beautiful environment of Achill Island. This is fuelled by a personal passion for the outdoors, again contrasting with the sense of obligation that drives Kenmare Resources' interactions, for example, or the sense of heritage which characterises O'Mahony's Bookshop.

Blackfield also does not report externally on its CSR activities, simply because of the perceived administrative burden, again highlighting the need for a simpler format of CSR reporting for smaller firms.

Case E

The HR Consultants

Nova Partners is a very new business. A two-person partnership, it was founded by Valerie O'Sullivan and Noreen Clifford in 2010 to offer HR services around recruitment, soft skills training, and training for performance. The firm is based in Cork, but is building up a client base all over Ireland.

Prior to forming the partnership, Noreen and Valerie worked in HR with multinational firms, in the University sector, and as independent consultants. Their services include training, coaching, recruitment, psychometric testing and general HR advice.

See www.mynovapartner.ie for further details.

I spoke to co-founder, Noreen Clifford, and she began by talking about what it was like to set up a new business in a recession.

Starting a Business in the Recession

Nova Partners is a HR consultancy, run by me and my partner, Valerie. The reason we started the business is partly because of the recession. Though both Valerie and I were individually self-employed as sole traders, work was becoming scarce. We wanted to have a company with a clear brand, so we decided to strike out in business together. The key thing we had in mind was that we wanted to really focus in on our customers, which is not that common, actually. Secondly, we wanted to be very clear and transparent about what we charge. We felt that this wasn't always clear in other businesses, and customers often found that difficult. Thirdly, we wanted to be involved in the whole area of business development, sourcing our own business, just getting out there and making an impact. That was about a year-and-a-half ago.

What CSR Means to Nova

When you're just starting, you don't really think of CSR in terms of calling it by that name. Our early focus was very much around: "What are our aims? What do we want to achieve? What are we here for? What will we be like as a business from our customers' perspective?" We didn't spend ages thinking about what CSR means, and how it would fit with us in the new venture.

Still, one of the first things we did was to start up a local networking group of other small businesses. Our basic idea was that we would all support each other. We researched other types of networks and found they have great reach and that a lot of small businesses get what they need to survive through that source. We asked around among people using these networks, and what came out was a feeling of having to come to every meeting of the network with a business referral for some other member of the group. This pressure to constantly come up with business referrals extended to putting pressure on the families of entrepreneurs to do their business only within the network, and we didn't want that immense pressure. You attend a meeting and during the preceding week you need to have referred at least one person to another member. While business can be generated this way, it seemed that, in some cases, it was all about the referral, and less about supporting each other. You have to show up to the meeting, or it's a black mark. It's very structured, very administrative.

It does work, definitely. You get business, but the pressure can be horrendous. It just didn't appeal to us. So, we launched Cork Connect with the idea of having a network of different businesses that would be able to support each other. We set up the group with an accountant, a solicitor and an insurance broker. We advised and supported each other, shared our problems, and so on. If something came up at work, you could lift the phone and ask someone who had dealt with that issue in the past. We were really involved, giving a lot to it at the start, and we also benefited a lot from our involvement. In the last few weeks, we've moved on from it because our business is a service, and it's harder for other small businesses to support us financially. We ran with it for a year, and now it's working well without us. We promote it still, and help out, but it's independent of us now. When we left, there were about 20 businesses. So, it was a good initiative, and we're very happy to have been involved.

In terms of CSR, we don't really focus on the environment. We don't consume an awful lot. Printing is the biggest thing, on the training side. The main thing for us, I suppose, is about relationships, and the people we're dealing with, being fair and transparent. That's something we were sure about from the beginning in terms of what kind of partnership or consultancy we wanted to be. There are a couple of things we do that not everybody does. We have a list of our services with the prices, and there is nothing hidden behind that. If we charge for a day's training, we don't charge design; we don't charge anything additional for tailoring it or going in and talking to the main organisers. We do all of those things, of course, but we only charge for the day of training. It's very common in this business for the pricing to be flexible, where more is charged if you think you would get more out of a customer. We both think it's unfair for companies not to see and understand what the bill will be, and we want to be very clear on terms and very clear on pricing.

We wouldn't have called that "corporate social responsibility", but it is how we wanted to operate. We just wanted to be clear, so our customers would never turn around and say: "You charged them so much, but you charged me that." We needed it to be very transparent and clear, and to feel at the end of the day that we hadn't exploited anybody, or cheated anyone. We are who we are. What we charge for the service doesn't change, whether you're a multinational or whether you're a small business.

The Origins of the Business's Ethos

Why we took this approach is definitely down to our own past experiences. We'd both worked in places where pricing was far less transparent. We would have felt uncomfortable with that, even though we weren't responsible. However, we were responsible for carrying out the work, and we knew about it. That's not comfortable, and it's not something you want to be associated with. It's a clash with our own values, and also not fair to the customer. Our ethos is very personal; it's about us as individuals, and the trust that we build through our own integrity.

On Challenges

We are only starting off, so we don't have too many choices of doing work for free or engaging in philanthropy. But one thing we do is pay people probably way too early. We pay suppliers immediately, whereas we don't get paid for weeks. That's something you don't do automatically, but it's definitely a value we both have. We know what it's like not to get paid and, often, we're sourcing business or a supply or printing from people we know, and we know they are small and need the money. Customers don't pay us early, but we pay our suppliers. We don't have huge overheads, and we keep them to a minimum, but anything we do buy, we pay for straight away. We are paid so late – it's almost like lending money!

A lot of the people that we buy from are people we know from the networking group. We also get some business from there, but not as much. The nature of the service we provide is such that smaller firms won't always pay a lot for it. So, the whole networking group is probably wrong for our model. We did toy with an idea of having a premium line for the HR advisory service, but we didn't like the idea of hidden charges, and it seemed a bit shady. It's back to the transparency thing again.

There are huge costs to our transparent pricing in terms of time, especially initially. Only some of our workdays are paydays. It's all about spending three days preparing for that one day. I feel that will stand to us in the long run. Already, I think it is beginning to, though it will probably take more than a year. It's only now that we're really delivering the service. It's only now that we're surveying our customers, asking them what they think of our service, what we could do better, and I think it will take a little time to get some feedback from them.

On Reporting

We don't really report our ethos of transparency on our website. We do say we're customer-focused, but so does everyone. I think the proof is in the pudding, and as our clients experience what we offer, that will get the message out. We don't look to CSR standards really, though that could be an interesting thing to do in the future.

On the Future

For the future, I'd love to employ people some day and to grow a little, but we don't want to get too big. I'm very happy with my life and the balance of my work. We're very happy to earn enough, if we can work out what 'enough' is. We have lots of people in the network who would be happy to work with us on a part-time basis, and I'd love to be able to do that a little bit more. If we get bigger, there would be a lot of work there, and we couldn't maintain it ourselves. So, definitely, again, it's one of the things we have to look at in the future.

If there was a change of leadership at the consultancy, things could change. Our ethos is very much built on relationships; it's very much about us, individually, and our own credibility. It could be hard to pass that on to new people. We need to be able to stand over what we do, and in the long-run, customers will see the difference. One of the things we struggled with is getting that message out there – "You can trust us." We do what we say we're going to do. Trust and customer focus and integrity are the things that are important to us.

This is a very new partnership, at a critical stage of building up its business, which is making a unique selling point of what could easily be labelled as CSR. They could make more of this by engaging in external CSR reporting, using the GRI template, and they probably will in the near future.

Their account is also interesting with regard to their difficulty in branding their personal integrity and honesty: "We do say we're customer-focused, but so does everyone." Again, this is where taking the time to report using an external template would help. There is a coherence about the approach taken by Nova, which may be down to their small numbers, just two partners. They have already articulated a vision of CSR for themselves, around honesty, reliability and transparency. This should make it easier for them to tell their story in a credible way, and generate some brand value from the integrity with which they operate.

Case F

The Outdoor Centre

Tollymore National Outdoor Centre is Northern Ireland's National Centre for Mountaineering and Canoeing Activities. It is funded and managed by Sport Northern Ireland and is located in Tollymore Forest, on the edge of the Mourne Mountains in County Down.

Sport Northern Ireland has three main strands: performance in sport, participation in sport, and facilities in sport. Tollymore falls within the themes of participation and facilities, helping Sport Northern Ireland to achieve the targets set out in their strategy document, *Sport Matters*.

The original Tollymore centre was built in the late 1970s as an outdoor pursuit centre, with a core business focused on building leadership skills for the outdoors. It started as a small business, with less than 10 staff, operating from a chalet-type building with outsourced catering. Despite the lack of resources, the centre was a leader in courses for canoeing and mountaineering.

It now operates in a spectacularly beautiful new building, opened in 2010, and designed to reflect the centre's ethos of sustainability.

See www.tollymore.com for more details.

I met Turlough Gorman of Sport Northern Ireland at the centre in October 2011, and he began by talking about what CSR means at Tollymore.

What CSR Means at Tollymore

At Tollymore, CSR is a lot about the environment and the outdoors, and making sure that it's protected. Our involvement really matters. Whether it is the numbers of people walking in the mountains, what sorts of activities take place in the water, all of that is largely influenced by small teams that sit in on committees and work in this area. The centre itself has CSR very much in mind in terms of the environmental aspect of the building. We looked at the use of rain water, wood burners, etc. The wood for the building is sourced locally, and we took care about things that had to be destroyed in the process of building. So, for instance, there was an old yew tree that had to be knocked down to build the centre, and the wood from that was harvested, and used to make the counter at reception, and the mantelpiece in the main hall. We were very keen that it be incorporated and, of course, it's beautiful.

Our staff are predominately local, so the people aspect of CSR is certainly present, as it would be with any business. For the community, we have sessions here at the centre; we use the large central room as a lecture theatre. We will have meetings just for the locals, letting them experience the building. We see it as something they have invested in.

A big aspect of work for the staff is the idea of Tollymore becoming a knowledge hotspot. All the staff here are busy with a number of activities on a strategic level. We don't just see them as deliverers; they are experts in different fields about which people can go to them for advice. It's all part of the service delivery; at least 20% of their job is furthering that knowledge, making the place a knowledge hotspot for outdoors. Obviously, the whole thing is publicly funded, so the core business should be in the North; however, a lot of our business comes from the South. The committees in this area are on an all-island basis, so the strategic involvement spreads beyond the six counties. We think in terms of people who are using the outdoors, and that cuts across the departmental aspect. Our stakeholders are not only the Department of Arts, Culture and Leisure, which is where we formally fit in, but all the other departments, whether it is Health, Education or Agricultural Development.

The Origins of Tollymore's Ethos

Why do we try to implement CSR? Because it works, I guess. There is a huge desire on the part of all of the staff to have it in place here. Lots of studies and models have proven the success of CSR. There is also an angle from the Government, in terms of their investment in the building. For any new building, they will have a number of stipulations. Renewable energy, for example, is one of the requirements, so we would have put in a business case for the standard we wanted to reach, and that business case would then be set against the regulations we have to comply with as a public building. I know that, in this building, we went far beyond the minimum required.

On Challenges, and Embedding the Culture

Of course there's a cost to most of these initiatives, especially when we're operating on an environmental level. For example, the building of this place was at a higher cost initially than it would have been with a more conventional design. It is only over a period of time that the cost can be dissipated, and it's not always easy to measure that. It might be by protecting the outdoors or recycling, whatever it is. Long term, we will find that we can recover some of the £5.2 million it cost to build the centre. I'm sure there are a lot of things we could have done a lot more cheaply in terms of actual upfront costs, but we wanted to look at the long-term sustainability.

We hold awareness sessions for the staff to make sure that the ethos permeates to them. We all devised the policy; it wasn't intended to be a document sitting in a cupboard. We have regular information sessions for staff on it. Sometimes, simple things work well. For instance, e-mails are sent around asking people to switch off their computers at night. We have security personnel on at night also, who ensure everything is switched off. The heating system is regulated. We switch off between the 1st of May and the 1st of October – our heat is completely off during that time. We monitor it during the day as well. We actually changed it because we had it on during lunch when a lot of people were out of the building, and we maybe didn't need it, so now we have it on only at the key times. We switch it off at 3pm because there is enough heat to keep us going till 6pm when the last people are leaving.

The people who work here now might go on to work elsewhere in the future. They'll have seen the practices here and I hope they might take that with them; I think actions speak louder than words. The policy is the words, in a way, but the action is the living out of the policy. The centre is very much built around the environment; that focus on the environment has to be embodied by all of us who work here, in or with the centre, and what we do every day at work.

On Reporting and Standards

We have reported our CSR on the website, but I guess we don't sell it enough. I recently carried out a progress report – where we are at the moment and where we need to be. The website is very important to publicise the centre and what we do, what we are about. That is certainly an area we can do a lot more in.

In terms of measuring the impact of what we do, we have an operational plan, which feeds into our business plan with Sport Northern Ireland. The economic situation has undoubtedly had an impact in terms of what we need to be about going forward. We have a reduction in schools coming through, a reduction in the corporations coming through. There are other providers who can do some of what we do, but at a lesser cost, for example, without accommodation. You see us coming in at £300, or someone who can do it for £120, and who do you go with? Everybody is thinking economically these days. And, then again, we are not all about competing with providers. Our bottom line is not just profit.

Leadership definitely matters. The director for participation and facilities based in Sports Northern Ireland is passionate about the outdoors. I think that very much comes across in what he has helped to create here in the facility and in the special nature of this building. He has known the business for as much as 12 years, and can compare the business now with what it was then. Largely because of the economic situation, the business has changed. The director certainly has retained his passion and drive for the outdoors, and he will ensure that there is strong support for continuing investment in this type of facility, and all that we do here.

On the Future

I think the business going forward will be more consumer-focused, but I guess it's the same with any business. It will be about meeting with expectations and finding where the demand is coming from. We need to stay responsive, while staying true to our principles. We have changed a great deal. It's interesting to look back at the business plan we set out in 2002 when we started planning what the new centre would look like, or even what we had planned about three years ago when it was approved. What we wanted to do then is not what we do now. We had to evolve to become what the customer wanted, to make sure the environment is protected, and to change the way people see the outdoors.

Tollymore is different from the privately-owned businesses featured in this book in that the rationale for their CSR activities is directly linked to the fact that they are a publicly-funded body. There is no distinction between the business and moral case; the reason for engaging in CSR is self-evident to them – "because it works".

The company is also interesting in having a single, clear focus to its CSR – the environment. This relates seamlessly with their core business of promoting the use and management of the outdoors. They see the community they serve as including all users of the outdoors, rather than being limited to those living in close proximity.

They consciously engender this ethos in all staff employed at the centre, through a range of awareness-raising initiatives, something that is less necessary in other small firms, which either have smaller staff numbers, longer-serving staff, or both.

The idea of sustainability at Tollymore is clearly linked to the long-term, especially in costing their innovative building. The centre is also interested in ideas of impact assessment, and measuring its overall environmental impact.

Overall, Tollymore provides a good example of how a larger organisation can achieve a very integrated and coherent CSR strategy by focusing on a single issue or group of issues, ideally ones that relate closely to the core business.

Case G

The Hotel

The Woodlands House Hotel is a family-run hotel located in a rural setting, just outside the pretty village of Adare, County Limerick. It is popular locally for weddings and parties, and attracts a wide range of business from all over the country and abroad. The hotel is situated on a large 44-acre site, sometimes used for corporate team-building activities.

The business was started by the Fitzgerald family as a small B&B in the 1970s, and gradually expanded over time, remaining in family owner-ship. It has operated as a hotel since 1983, and now has 94 bedrooms, a conference centre, leisure centre and spa, and employs more than 150 people. Three of the founders' four children work directly in the business, and the family also operates a second hotel in Cork City.

See www.woodlands-hotel.ie for more details.

I spoke to the founder, Mary Fitzgerald in 2011, and she began by describing the key elements of CSR in the Woodlands House Hotel.

What CSR means to the Woodlands House Hotel

For us, CSR is mostly about customers, employees and the community. We also give to charity, both in time and in money, but caring for people, that's what matters. It's very important for us all to give back to the community. On a personal level, I am involved with dozens of organisations locally. That's my bit for the community, for society. My staff can see me getting involved per-sonally like that, so it sets the pace. It's about openness and willingness to give without always getting. It's about doing as much as we can for people, and treating everyone with respect.

We're careful about small things, like getting security in. We don't use external security very much, because it can sometimes be seen as antagonis-tic. They are used to working in town, in nightclubs or whatever, and it's different in the country. There is also a responsibility in serving alcohol, which is really all about training for the staff. The training is available very easily, and all our people have been trained. The staff implements all our responsibilities really, even for simple things, like making sure the floor is cleaned so that someone doesn't fall. Accidents do happen, so we need to maintain this culture of taking responsibility. It's up to the leader to put it in place, especially with junior workers.

Food matters to us. I wouldn't give my customers anything to eat that I wouldn't like to eat myself. There is no way I would tolerate MSG, for instance. If I know it would be bad for me, why would I use it in the hotel? The people in my kitchen know that if you wouldn't serve it to your family, then we don't serve it to our customers. We have no great strategy, but if you want to come and work with us, this is the type of culture you will be in.

Now and then, I'll go into the kitchen and say hello to everybody, see how they all are doing. If someone is busy peeling potatoes or something, and they need me to put something on for them, I will, and I'll chat away to any of them. It's that respect that matters. My staff are not just numbers, and they won't be treated badly. Getting everyone who works with us to respect one another, I think that would be a dominant part of our corporate culture.

On the Origins of the Business's Ethos

We came from a farming background, where you cared and you shared. My husband came from a similar kind of stock, where you put yourself above and beyond the call of duty, because you had to. When we were starting off, we knew that a place like ours would have to do things so much better than the established hotels, just to get our legs under the table, because of the reputation that our competitors have built up over the years. We decided to work much harder on our credibility to deliver.

On Making it Part of the Culture

It's very important to think about how we get that message across to our staff about the openness and the honesty. While I want the ethos to spread, from the top down and all through the organisation, a lot also comes down to the training, and how we mentor the staff, so that the customer is in their thought processes. In my opinion, mentoring is much more important than training.

Training is task orientated – they must know the basic tasks, and have the soft skills. It's important with mentoring that you give the person rope, that you allow them to do their own thing.

We have great staff. I have people working for years with me who would take a bullet for the business. There's loyalty there to ideas that started as personal to us and then became part of the culture for everyone. When developing a business, it's amazing how important your personal input is to the culture. It's up to you, as a leader, to develop the ethos.

On Challenges

Not everything has worked out for us, however. A year or two back we started allotments in a field alongside the hotel. It was a nice idea – people would come and grow things there, and we would buy anything they wanted to sell. We have the land, and we could provide a market. We got an expert out on Sundays to offer help to anyone who wanted advice. The idea was for it to be a social thing, not just a way of supplying us with produce, we wanted to create something for people. This year, though, demand has disappeared. Before, you couldn't get allotments easily, but now they're available and very close to the city. People also realised that they are very hard work, so that didn't work out as planned. This year, we are using some of our own allotments directly. This can be a stressful job as well and the allotment gives us all a chance to get outside for a quarter of an hour or so. One of the local charities is using one as well, so there is still a value from the project outside of the hotel.

Growing a business brings risks at different stages, especially to your ethos. When your business is small, you can to put your hands around it, and hold it. You know where everything is, and how everything is done. In 1999, when we built our leisure centre, I thought we had arrived. We had a leisure centre, 94 bedrooms, which was a whole new level of business. Our customers were becoming more affluent. There was a lot for me to learn about their needs. For instance, I couldn't understand the demand for the crèche, because if I was away with my family, because we worked so hard all year, I would want to spend all the holiday time with my kids. Still, through my involvement in the Irish Hotels Federation,[85] I knew where we were going. I knew what we needed.

---

[85] www.ihf.ie.

But the staff at the time weren't able to deliver my vision. We hadn't prepared well enough to bring in all this new stuff. I remember we went on a family holiday to Tralee and when we came back things were not good – there were even complaints, which shocked me, because that had never happened before. So we sat down and weighed things up. I said: "OK, if I want to have my new extended business, I need to work out how to make this happen." The trouble is that as we moved to that next step in our development, we weren't able to deliver the same quality we had previously. For me, personally, I had been in control of every aspect of the business before, but now I felt I had to let go of control. So, we hired a consultant, and on the first day he said to me: "Are you prepared to lose three-quarters of your team?" This caused a lot of stress at the time, but it worked. It got us back on the ladder again.

Now we have come to the point where we have different challenges. We focus on our ability to pay our debts and our ability to be completely market-driven, not to be overshadowed by the big hotel chains in Limerick. How can we grow and still keep the personal touch? There is also a need for transparency and honesty and real clarity. The internet has changed the way people think about pricing. Someone sitting at home on a Sunday can ring up and say: "When I checked you had two rooms left at €150, but I can go elsewhere and only pay €100." We need to be careful about how we deal with this whole thing of clarity, our responsibility to our customer, how they treat us and how we treat them. That part might be a bit easier for us than for our competitors, because we'd always had it as part of the way we work.

On the Future

Whether this ethos will pass down to the next generation or not I couldn't be sure, but I think it will. Part of that is about how you treat your children and your grandchildren, rearing them to respect other people. Respect is at the root of it: you need respect for your staff, and they need to respect their work colleagues, especially people coming in at the bottom end of the business. In turn, that translates to respect for the customer. You don't want anything to happen to your customer because they're too scarce. You have to look after your customer like you'd look after your own mother. We tell this to our staff all the time.

With us, what you see is what you get. We grew our business around the delivery of an honest product. People feel very comfortable with us. People see us as credible people standing over our product who say "This is what we do" and "This is how it is". There's always that open honesty about what we do.

> The Woodlands House Hotel business is built on strong family values which inform their CSR strategy. The values of the business are very personal and grounded – the kind of *second-nature* CSR that can be a real strength for smaller firms. Again, we see the importance of employees to achieving and maintaining this – "having the right people working for us".
>
> In this context, it is interesting to see the importance placed on mentoring employees and inculcating the ethos of the organisation in them. There is a fine distinction made between training and mentoring. Significantly, the most challenging time recalled was when the business was growing, and every aspect could no longer be personally controlled by the owner.
>
> Again we see the common theme of respect coming through, expressed as in the case of KPS Colourprint (see **Case A**) as relating to the respect management have for employees as well as respect for the customers. The owners recognise that their values could be a key advantage in competing with larger, less personal hotel chains. In this context, CSR could be a selling point for the Woodlands House Hotel.
>
> It could be useful for them to implement reporting under the Global Reporting Initiative guidelines as described in **Chapter 5**. These would enable them to produce a simple, honest and tailored report of their approach to CSR.

Case H

The School Lunch Provider

Carambola is a Limerick-based company founded in 2003 by Colm O'Brien and his wife Aideen, which supplies school lunches to thousands of school-going children across Ireland every day. The company operates from a premises in Annacotty, County Limerick, and employs almost 60 people. Much of their business comes from the DEIS program,[86] which deals with disadvantaged schools, and currently Carambola holds almost 20% of that market at primary school level. In 2012, Carambola will deliver its 10 million[th] school lunch in Ireland.

Carambola focuses on offering healthy lunch options. The company also works to promote awareness among children of healthy lifestyle choices, engaging children through their mascots 'Cara' and 'Bola', around which a nutrition and health-based board game has been developed.

See www.carambola.ie for more details.

I spoke to founder Colm O'Brien in 2011, and he began by providing some context to the setting up of the company, and describing what CSR means in Carambola.

On Context, and What CSR means in Carambola

Carambola was born out of our previous business, the Bewley's Café in Cruise's Street, Limerick. When that business ended, it was a tough time for me and my wife. I feel we were blessed with the opportunity to reinvent ourselves, and we found ourselves in a space which we had never imagined:

---

[86] DEIS is an Irish Government programme, Delivering Equality of Opportunity in Schools, which targets schools taking children from disadvantaged communities. Details are available at www.education.ie/servlet/blobservlet/DEIS_action_plan_on_educational_inclusion.pdf?language=EN; last accessed 15 May 2012.

feeding kids, especially in disadvantaged areas. We expanded because we found we were able to create jobs, and we felt that if we could do that, then we should.

We engaged in an education programme for children because one of the biggest problems facing Ireland and the world, certainly the developed world, is the obesity of children. So we developed a programme for teaching awareness about what makes a healthy lifestyle. In fact, this has become our mission. I feel that we are in a very positive space where we are doing a very good job with a very good food product, and we are giving back to the communities with which we trade. We are supplying about 100 schools in the country now; that's up to 20,000 children in a given day. Whatever money each school spends with us, we then donate a portion of that back to the school. We encourage them to donate it to local charities, ideally child-centred charities, though we leave the choice up to the school.

We maintain high standards. We follow the best practice in terms of employment law, with our employees. We only deal with recognised companies. Being in the food game poses its own challenges: it is vital that we have transparency and traceability all the way, right back to the source. Every company we deal with has to step up to the mark in terms of food safety. That means making choices. We can't make decisions on what to include in our lunches simply based on what we can buy for the right price.

We have kept a very high standard from the beginning. We take the moral high ground from a nutrition perspective. When someone comes to us with an idea for a product, the first thing we do is pass it to our nutritionist. She decides if the product is nutritionally good, and we base our decision on hers. There could be too much sugar or salt, or whatever it might be in the product, and if so, we won't touch it. This is something we do regardless of price. Products go to our nutritionist first, and only then to our purchasing people. If those two are happy then we test it in the market place.

On Challenges

Our approach to selecting products for inclusion in the lunch packs certainly has its downside. For example, one competitor doesn't offer pure fruit juice, substituting water for the juice option. Hydration is very important ,of course, but we find that, given the choice, about one-third of kids will drink water and two-thirds will prefer juice. Those drinking juice are getting more nutrition. However, water is 60% the price of juice, so we feel a bit penalised for sticking to the spirit of this Government-sponsored school lunch programme when others out there are bending the rules to suit the bottom line.

Our approach and ethos could also give us a strategic advantage in the market, but it's a tricky one to communicate. Most of the schools that we deal with have been with us for many years. They love what we do and what we stand for, and they wouldn't easily change away from Carambola to another supplier because of the fact that we have never let them down. Our ethos is there; our standards are there.

Making the Ethos Part of the Culture

I think the mood of an organisation comes from the top, and it's important to communicate that to everyone. We have a very open organisation, and the way we put it is: we are interested in "feeding Johnny". *'Johnny Moloney'* represents every child out there. We do whatever we have to, to ensure Johnny gets fed properly. In fact one of our real challenges is that if we don't do our job right on any given day, some child really will go hungry. That is the fundamental, bottom line in our business. If we forget Johnny's lunch, he doesn't eat. In certain cases, not in all cases, that might be the best meal that Johnny would get that day because a lot of these kids come from disadvantaged areas. I don't believe we have ever let Johnny down, though we have had some hairy moments. We have had to send vans to Dublin or to Galway or Cork because we mislaid a tray of lunches. Johnny must get fed. Everything else, including the net profit bottom line comes after that. If we don't feed Johnny we don't deserve to make money and I think everybody in the organisation understands that.

We are actually interested in feeding Johnny. We feel we offer much more than a sandwich in a bag. We offer a nutrition programme. A whole education programme around why children, particularly disadvantaged children, need to eat properly.

On the Changing Nature of CSR

We started out with food. To be honest, on Day One, it really had nothing to do with nutrition. When we found ourselves in this business, it was built on the failure of our café. We just needed to put bread on the table. Thankfully, we fell across this opportunity and started to take it seriously. Then Rachel

Mescall Fitzpatrick joined us as our nutritional advisor five years ago. She was the one who began to talk to us about the importance of nutrition. Before that, we were unaware of it all ourselves. I am now a huge fan of what we as an organisation can do. So, our mission has evolved: on Day 1 our mission was to pay the rent, and now it has become the promotion of healthy lifestyle awareness for all children, not just those we deal with.

From early on, Rachel decided that it was worthwhile being in the schools talking to the kids. At least once a year we are in each of our schools, offering training sessions. Whether in a classroom or a *halla beag*, it's a full interaction with the children. For junior kids, we talk about the magic energy that they get from eating good food or from doing the right thing.

In fact, we recently invented a board game that teaches kids about these issues. It's called the *Carambola Board Game*. The subtitle is *Cara and Bola Magic Energy Game*, and it's an interesting new development for us. You roll the dice and move along, making choices – an apple instead of chocolate, or helping in the kitchen instead of watching television. We try to teach kids they are in charge of their own decisions. Even seven or eight-year-olds are in a position to decide between a fizzy drink or pure fruit juice. Too often, they make the wrong one. We try to teach them that if they make the right choice, water or juice, they have more energy to go and do the things they want to do. If they put the wrong stuff in, or make the wrong decision in terms of habits, not to do homework, etc., they know deep down that it's not the right thing to do and they lose that momentum. We are very enthusiastic about what we can do with this. There are lots of kids out there who don't know this stuff, and this is a fun way for them to get the message that they're maybe not getting at home.

Again this all comes from our mission to promote healthy lifestyle awareness for children. The feedback has been great. There is a real market in that seven to eight-year-old bracket. I'm excited about that. We will sell it, commercially. CSR is important, but we also are in business to make money. We are very happy to give back but we are also very happy to build business. I'm very much interested to see how this develops, to see how the brand performs. Everything we try to do is linked to the brand.

On Standards, and the Origins of the Business's Ethos

We focus on doing the right thing and the motivation for that comes from within, not from outside. I didn't even know there were CSR standards.

I think what we do comes from that thing of feeling blessed. There are people in far worse positions then we are. So we don't report what we do yet. We don't have a CSR section on our website. I imagine in time, if we go public, that may become part of our sales pitch, but that's a bit down the road.

This ethos of the business, at this moment in time, is very dependent on our leadership. I think if anyone else bought it over he or she might look at it differently. But, that said, I think there may be enough of a spirit engendered in the team here of wanting to feed 'Johnny' and do the right thing for this to last. Someone coming in trying to change that would meet with a lot of resistance.

It has been difficult when we see other firms with lower nutritional standards winning business precisely because they have been unscrupulous. We can say that it's not fair and it's true – and it's not fair – but we aren't going to join them. I have always believed that if you do the job right, the money will flood in. We work to do the job right first in the hopes that there is money behind it. That's why we try stuff, we try to see if there is a market for the idea, like the board game, and we hope there is money behind it.

It's good business to do the right thing. We never have to look over our shoulder. We don't try to get away with stuff. The universal laws would dictate that if you do the right thing you get the result, in the long term.

Again, we see the personal values of the founders of a business being brought to bear strategically, in this case when the business was set up following the closure of a previous venture.

The personality of the owners is reflected in the way in which CSR has developed and changed over time for the company. It is essentially an entrepreneurial sort of development, and the company has moved up along the stages of CSR described in **Exhibit 16**. There is clear engagement with stakeholders, and an ambition to transform the industry to some extent.

At the same time, there is no real awareness of CSR standards *per se* in the business, although high standards are adhered to in other areas, such as food safety and employment law. Interestingly, CSR reporting is seen primarily as something that might be useful if the company were sold, or if we go 'public'. However, some external reporting of CSR could be useful to Carambola now, since they are struggling to communicate their commitment to high nutritional standards: "Our approach and ethos could also give us a strategic advantage in the market, but it's a tricky one to communicate."

References and Resources

Audi, R. (2009). *Business Ethics and Ethical Business*. Oxford University Press.

Beckett. L. (2012). *Foxconn by the Numbers*. Huffington Post ProPublica, January 2012.

Blowfield, M. and Murray, A. (2008). *Corporate Responsibility: a Critical Introduction*. Oxford University Press.

Cragg, W., Schwartz, M. S. and Weitzner, D. (2009). Corporate Social Responsibility, from *The Library of Corporate Responsibilities*. Ashgate Publishing Ltd, Surrey.

Craig Smith, N. (2003). "Corporate Social Responsibility: Not Whether, but How?" London Business School Centre for Marketing Working Paper No. 03-701, April 2003.

Dowling Daley, M. (1989). *Irish Laws*. Appletree Press, Belfast.

Drucker, P. (1974). *Management: Tasks, Responsibilities, Practices*.William Heinemann Ltd, London.

Drucker, P. (1986). *The Frontiers of Management: Where Tomorrow's Decisions are Being Shaped Today*. Truman Talley Books/E.D.Dutton, New York.

EC (2008). European Commission Enterprise and Industry. SBA Fact Sheet – Ireland. Available online at http://ec.europa.eu/enterprise/policies/sme/facts-figures-analysis/performance-review/files/countries-sheets/2008/ireland_en.pdf.

Elkington, J. (1997). *Cannibals with Forks: Triple Bottom Line of 21st Century Business*. Capstone Publishers. October 1997.

Erisman, A. (2004). "Don Flow: Ethics at Flow Automotive." *Ethix* (34), April 2004.

Freeman, E. (1984). *Strategic Management: a Stakeholder Approach*. Pitmann Series in Business and Public Policy.

Friedman, M. (1970). "The Social Responsibility of Business is to Increase its Profits". *New York Times Magazine,* September 1970.

Frost, S. and Burnett, M. (2007). *Case study: the Apple iPod in China, Corporate Social Responsibility and Environmental Management*, 14, (2007).

Hawken, P. (1994). *The Ecology of Commerce: a Declaration of Sustainability*. Harper Business.

ITGLWF (2011). Report by the International Textile Garment and Leather Workers' Federation. An Overview of Working Conditions in Sportswear Factories in Indonesia, Sri Lanka & the Philippines. Available online at http://www.itglwf.org/lang/en/documents/ITGLWFSportswearReport2011.pdf.

Jenkins, H. (2006). "Small Businesses Champions for Corporate Social Responsibility". *Journal of Business Ethics*, 67, 241–256.

Jensen, M. and Meckling, W. (1976). "Theory of the Firm: Managerial Behavior, Agency Costs and Ownership Structure". *Journal of Financial Economics*, October, 1976, 3(4), 305–360.

Kerrigan, G. (2006). "Making a killing on the market is no big deal". *Sunday Independent*, November 12, 2006.

Lenssen, G., Perrin, F., Tencati, A. and Lacy, P. (2007). "Corporate responsibility, strategic management and the stakeholder view of the firm". *Corporate Governance: the international journal of business in society*, 7 (4), 344–354.

Jiao Luo, J., Meier, S. and Oberholzer-Gee, F. (2012). No News Is Good News: CSR Strategy and Newspaper Coverage of Negative Firm Events. HBS Working Paper Number: 12-091, April 2012.

Mandl, I. and Dorr, A. (2005). CSR and Competitiveness – European SMEs' Good Practice – Consolidated European Report. KMU Forschung Austria, 2005.

McElhaney, K. (2008). *Just Good Business: The Strategic Guide to Aligning Corporate Responsibility and Brand*. Berrett-Koehler Publishers.

Mirvis, P. and Googins, B. (2006). *Stages of Corporate Citizenship*. Boston College Center for Citizenship Monograph (2006).

O'Brien, J. (2009). Corporate Social Responsibility, from *The Library of Corporate Responsibilities*. Ashgate Publishing Ltd, Surrey.

Poliszcuk, L. and Sakashita, M. (2010). Japan, *The World Guide to CSR: a country-by-country analysis of corporate sustainability and responsibility*, edited by Wayne Visser and Nick Tolhust. Greenleaf Publishing, Sheffield, 2010, 223–229.

Posnick, L., Kim, H. and Bailey, C. (2002). "Ask the Regulators – Bottled Water Regulation and the FDA". *Food Safety Magazine*, September 2002.

Ramesh, R. (2010). "Food Standards Agency to be abolished by health secretary". *The Guardian*, July 12, 2010.

Schmidt, E. and Varian, H. (2005). "Google: 10 Golden Rules". *Newsweek*, 2 December, 2005.

Smith, G., Hoag, F. and Fedelman, D. (2003). "Company Codes of Conduct and International Standards: an Analytical Comparison". World Bank and IFC report, October 2003.

Smith, C. and Lenssen, G. (Eds) (2009). *Mainstreaming Corporate Social Responsibility*. John Wiley and Sons, Sussex.

Spence, M. (1973). "Job Market Signalling". *Quarterly Journal of Economics*, 87 (3). August 1973.

Stabile, C. (2000). "Nike, social responsibility, and the hidden abode of production". *Critical Studies in Media Communication*, 17 (2), 2000.

Sulik, G. (2010). *Pink Ribbon Blues: How Breast Cancer Culture Undermines Women's Health*. New York: Oxford University Press.

Tax Strategy (2006). "The SME Sector in Ireland – Information paper". Tax Strategy Group Paper 06/14 September 2006 available online at http://taxpolicy.gov.ie/wp-content/uploads/2011/04/0614.pdf.

Wan-Jan, W. S. (2006). "Defining corporate social responsibility". *Journal of Public Affairs* (Special Issue: Corporate Social Responsibility), 6(3–4). August – November 2006.

Index

advertising 35, 42, 49
Aer Lingus 22
Airlink 52
altruism 109, 111
Amnesty International 25
Anderson, Ray 84–5
Apple 46
Audi, R. 14
Australia 63

Ballygowan 8, 51
Ben & Jerry's Ice Cream 66
benchmarking 54, 57, 62
Blackfield Clothing and Surf School
    31, 36, 47, 72, 77, 113–17
Blowfield, M. 18
Body Shop 8
branding 8, 34, 119, 123, 140
Brannigan, Gerry 47, 72, 77, 113–17
breast cancer 8, 50–51
Brehon Laws 17
bribery 42–3, 56
bullying 42
Burnett, M. 46
business ethics 6, 12–15, 71
Business in the Community
    Ireland (BITCI) 38, 61

Cadbury 18–20, 48, 61
capital markets 85–6
Carambola Ltd 45, 72, 75, 137–42
carbon credits 32–3, 34, 66
carbon footprint 31–3, 34, 66–7
cause-related marketing 8,
    49–52, 66
CERES 25

charitable donations 8, 9–10, 18, 22,
    49, 131, 138
charities 8, 15, 22, 24–5, 49–52, 133
child labour 11, 19, 42, 56, 57, 58
China 46
Clifford, Noreen 72, 119–23
Code of Hammurabi 17
codes of conduct 8, 12
codes of practice 23, 26, 48
competition 29–30, 79
community 4, 5, 7, 8, 18, 24, 25,
    35–9, 42, 49, 68, 70–71, 73,
    99–101, 102–3, 104, 106,
    108–9, 111, 113–14, 117, 126,
    129, 131, 133, 138
community outreach 35, 73
consultation 24, 32, 36, 42, 63, 64,
    101, 102–3
Corcoran, Deirdre 63, 99–106
corporate citizenship 6–7
corporate responsibility 7
corporate social responsibility
    aspects of 8–10
    business arguments for 15–16
    current trends 22–6
    definition 3–6
    evolution in 82–4, 141
    future trends 79–87
    history of 17–22
    moral arguments for 12–15
    reporting *see* reporting
    responsibilities involved 27–52,
        76–8
    in SMEs 70–78
    standards and regulation *see*
        standards

corruption 42–4, 56, 84
Craig Smith, N. 58

Davis, Keith 20
DEIS programme 137
deontological approach 12
Diageo 9
Dickens, Charles 18
disability 8
discrimination 39, 40, 56
Disney 8
diversity 39, 42
Dorr, A. 71, 73, 75, 76
Dowling Daley, Mary 17
Drucker, Peter 21

economic responsibilities 27–31
Edelman Trust Barometer 80
education 18, 36, 42, 58, 101, 109,
    115, 138, 140
Elkington, John 6, 7
employment provision 35, 83, 103,
    104, 109, 113–14, 116–17, 138
energy 15, 31, 35, 84, 85, 126, 127
environment 6, 7, 8, 9, 11, 12, 15, 25,
    31–5, 56, 63, 74, 84–5, 95, 97,
    103, 105, 115, 116, 117, 120,
    125–7, 129
equality 39, 40, 42
Erisman, A. 29
Ethical Corporation 62
ethics *see* business ethics
ethos 8, 14, 42, 72, 73, 75, 91, 92, 93,
    95–6, 97, 109, 116, 121, 123,
    126, 127, 129, 132–3, 134–5,
    139, 140–41
extortion 43, 56

Facebook 67
fair competition 29

Fairtrade 13, 47, 54, 68, 77, 114, 115
families 40, 41, 42, 107–8
financial reporting 6, 67
Finland 76
Fitzgerald, Mary 14, 40, 48, 73,
    131–5
Fitzpatrick, Rachel Mescall 139–40
Flow, Don 29
Flow Automotive 29
forced labour 11, 12, 15–16, 19, 56,
    61, 64
Ford 51
Forest Stewardship Council 95, 97
Foxconn 46
Freeman, Edward 21
Friedman, Milton 20, 27, 49
Frost, S. 46

GAP 76, 77
Garnier, Jean-Paul 58
Germany 74
GlaxoSmithKline 14, 58
Global Reporting Initiative (GRI)
    56–60, 62, 65, 82, 97, 123, 135
global warming 31
Googins, Bradley 82–3
Google 8
Gorman, Turlough 72, 125–9
governance 42–4
Guardian, The 8
Guinness 9

Habitat for Humanity 52
Harkin-Engel Protocol 19
Hawken, Paul 84
health 24, 37, 58, 101–2, 104, 137,
    138, 140
health and safety 39, 57, 96,
    105, 132
hello money 31, 43

HelpX 113–14, 116

human rights 25, 41–2, 47–8, 56, 76, 116, 117

ILO Declaration on Fundamental Principles and Rights at Work 55

impact assessments 81, 128, 129

Imphala 66–7, 68

Industrial Revolution 18

Innocent Drinks 65–6, 68

InterContinental Hotels Group 34

Interface Carpets 39, 83, 84–5

International Labour Organisation (ILO) 19, 39–40, 46, 55, 56, 57–8, 77

International Organisation for Standardisation (ISO) 60–61

Irish Aid 102

ISO 26000 60–61

ISTAT 52

Japan 17–18

Jensen, M. 4

Jerome, David 34

Jiao Luo, J. 46

job security 39, 96

Kelly, Peter 41

Kenmare Resources 22, 24, 36, 37, 63, 71, 82, 99–106

Kimberley Process 23, 48, 61

KPS Colourprint 40, 72, 93–7

labelling 13, 45, 47, 50–51, 54–5, 61

leaders 8, 12, 14, 73, 91, 128, 132–3, 141

legal requirements 5, 39, 45, 63–4, 82

Lenssen, G. 3, 9

local community *see* community

long-termism 31, 38–9, 48, 53, 92, 105, 106, 122, 127, 129, 141

LR Gebäudereinigung 74

McElhaney, Kellie 21

Mackay, Graham 11

Manchester City Football Club 68

Mandl, I. 71, 73, 75, 76

marketing 8, 28, 33, 34, 37, 49–52

Marubeni 18

Meckling, W. 4

mentoring 40, 133, 135

minimum wage 5, 39

Mirvis, Philip 82–3

morale 41, 75

Motorola 46

Mozambique 24, 36, 63, 99–106

Murray, A. 18

National Standards Authority of Ireland (NSAI) 61

Neste Oil 34

networking 120, 122

Nigeria 37

Nike 76

Nokia 46

non-governmental organisations (NGOs) 22, 23–5, 59

Norway 74–5

Nova Partners 29, 72, 119–23

Novo Nordisk 67

O'Brien, Colm 72, 75, 137–42

Olympus 55

O'Mahony, David 35, 70, 71, 107–11

O'Mahony's Bookshop 35, 36, 70, 71, 107–11

Organisation for Economic
    Cooperation and Development
    (OECD) 59

packaging 15, 31, 35, 59, 84
partnering 22–5, 82, 101–2, 106
Patagonia 29–30
philanthropy 18, 20, 35, 37, 49, 52,
    82, 83
Pinkwashing 50–51
pollution 15, 31
Posnik, L. 51
pricing 14, 28–9, 72, 119, 121,
    122, 134
product quality 10, 45, 94
product safety 45
profit 6, 15, 19, 27–8, 82, 83, 116
Programme for the Endorsement of
    Forest Certification 95, 97
promotion 39
Protu AS 74–5

Rabobank 68–9
Ramesh, R. 61
recession 21, 28, 30, 31, 40–41, 93–4,
    96, 119
recycling 31, 34, 59, 84–5, 95
recruitment 8, 39, 91, 94–5
redundancies 40–41
regulation 54–62
reporting 6, 7, 56–7, 59–60, 63–9,
    71–6, 82, 83, 84, 97, 99, 103,
    106, 110–11, 115, 117, 122,
    123, 127–8, 135, 141–2
reputation 29, 30, 31, 34, 35,
    37, 44, 45–6, 49, 63, 68,
    71, 94
respect 41, 42, 92, 93, 96, 97, 106,
    131, 132, 134, 135

responsibilities
    for causes 49–52
    economic 27–31
    to employees and human rights
        39–42
    environmental 31–5
    governance 42–4
    to the local community 35–9
    for product safety and quality 45
    in SMEs 76–8
    for supply chains 45–8, 76–8
rights-based ethics 14
Rio Declaration on Environment
    and Development 55
Romania 75
Royal Dutch Shell 37
rules-based consequentialism 13

SA8000 47, 60, 68
SAB Miller 11
Salmon, Brendan 40, 42, 72, 93–7
sanction 54–5, 62
sanpo yoshi 18
SC Icemenerg SA 75
Schmidt, Eric 8
second nature 92, 111, 135
SEED Initiative 62
shareholders 6, 9, 15, 20,
    21, 103
signalling theory 64–5, 68, 69
SMEs 14, 35, 45–6, 56, 60, 66, 67,
    70–78
Smith, C. 9 ,12
Social Accountability Accreditation
    Services (SAAS) 60
Social Accountability International
    (SAI) 47–8, 60
social capital 37, 49, 63
social media 67, 81–2

Socially Responsible Investment funds (SRIs) 85–6
soft law 23, 26, 48
'Songbird Friendly' labelling 47, 54–5
South Africa 25, 58, 66–7, 86
Spain 76
Spence, Michael 64–5, 68, 69
sponsorship 9–10, 15, 35, 42, 49
Sport Northern Ireland 125, 128
Stabile, C. 76
stakeholders 4, 5, 6, 8, 9, 15, 21, 63, 81, 83, 103, 126
standards 54–62, 72–3, 82, 95, 97, 115, 122, 127–8, 140, 141
Starbucks 5, 77
Sulik, G. 51
supply chains 9, 19–20, 22, 29–30, 33–4, 40, 45–8, 64, 76–8
sustainability 7, 10, 31, 32, 34–5, 47, 57, 64–9, 75, 85, 86, 95, 104, 125–7, 129
sweatshops 30, 76–7, 115

taxation 29, 30, 82, 83, 114, 117
Timberland 67
Tollymore National Outdoor Centre 33, 36, 72, 125–9
traceability 48, 138
traction 54–5, 61, 62
training 39, 40, 74, 100, 101, 132, 133, 135
transparency 15, 39, 91, 119, 121, 122, 123, 134, 138
Transparency International 44
transport 15, 31, 35, 84
triple bottom line 6, 18, 86

trust 9, 63, 71, 75, 79–81, 123
Tudor Rose 56
Twitter 67, 69

United Kingdom 18, 38, 56, 61
United Nations Children's Fund (UNICEF) 22–3, 56
United Nations Convention Against Corruption 55
United Nations Global Compact 41–2, 55–6, 59, 65, 82
United States 46, 50, 51, 52, 63–4, 76, 84
Universal Declaration of Human Rights 41, 55
utilitarianism 13

values 8, 12, 14, 73, 75, 91, 92, 96, 109, 121, 132, 135, 141
virtue-based ethics 14
volunteering 8

wages 5, 39, 42, 57–8, 76
Walgreens 8
Wan-Jan, W.S. 9
waste 9, 31, 35, 59, 84–5
water resources 11, 84
water rights 42, 84
Westpac 68
Whirlpool 52
Woodlands House Hotel 14, 40, 48, 73, 131–5
work-life balance 74–5
working age 39, 40, 58
working conditions 18–20, 29–30, 39, 42, 45–6, 75, 76–7
working hours 39, 40, 57, 76